MACMILLAN MODE

General Editor: Norman Page

MACMILLAN MODERN NOVELISTS

Published titles

ALBERT CAMUS Philip Thody
FYODOR DOSTOEVSKY Peter Conradi
WILLIAM FAULKNER David Dowling
GUSTAVE FLAUBERT David Roe
E. M. FORSTER Norman Page
WILLIAM GOLDING James Gindin
GRAHAM GREENE Neil McEwan
HENRY JAMES Alan Bellringer
D. H. LAWRENCE G. M. Hyde
DORIS LESSING Ruth Whittaker
MALCOLM LOWRY Tony Bareham
GEORGE ORWELL Valerie Meyers
ANTHONY POWELL Neil McEwan
MARCEL PROUST Philip Thody
BARBARA PYM Michael Cotsell
SIX WOMEN NOVELISTS Merryn Williams
MURIEL SPARK Norman Page
JOHN UPDIKE Judie Newman
EVELYN WAUGH Jacqueline McDonnell
H. G. WELLS Michael Draper
VIRGINIA WOOLF Edward Bishop

Forthcoming titles

MARGARET ATWOOD Coral Ann Howells
SAUL BELLOW Paul Hyland
IVY COMPTON-BURNETT Janet Godden
JOSEPH CONRAD Owen Knowles
GEORGE ELIOT Alan Bellringer
F. SCOTT FITZGERALD John Whitley
JOHN FOWLES James Acheson
ERNEST HEMINGWAY Peter Messent
CHRISTOPHER ISHERWOOD Stephen Wade
JAMES JOYCE Richard Brown
NORMAN MAILER Michael Glenday
THOMAS MANN Martin Travers
V. S. NAIPAUL Bruce King
PAUL SCOTT G. K. Das
PATRICK WHITE Mark Williams

MACMILLAN MODERN NOVELISTS

ANTHONY POWELL

Neil McEwan

MACMILLAN

First published 1991

Published by
MACMILLAN EDUCATION LTD
Houndmills, Basingstoke, Hampshire RG21 2XS
and London
Companies and representatives
throughout the world

Typeset by BP Integraphics, Ltd., Bath, Avon

Printed in Hong Kong

British Library Cataloguing in Publication Data
McEwan, Neil
Anthony Powell—(Macmillan modern novelists).
1. Fiction in English. Powell, Anthony, 1905–
I. Title
823.912
ISBN 0–333–49711–2 (hc)
ISBN 0–333–49712–0 (pbk)

Contents

General Editor's Preface

The death of the novel has often been announced, and part of the secret of its obstinate vitality must be its capacity for growth, adaptation, self-renewal and self-transformation: like some vigorous organism in a speeded-up Darwinian ecosystem, it adapts itself quickly to a changing world. War and revolution, economic crisis and social change, radically new ideologies such as Marxism and Freudianism, have made this century unprecedented in human history in the speed and extent of change, but the novel has shown an extraordinary capacity to find new forms and techniques and to accommodate new ideas and conceptions of human nature and human experience, and even to take up new positions on the nature of fiction itself.

In the generations immediately preceding and following 1914, the novel underwent a radical redefinition of its nature and possibilities. The present series of monographs is devoted to the novelists who created the modern novel and to those who, in their turn, either continued and extended, or reacted against and rejected, the traditions established during that period of intense exploration and experiment. It includes a number of those who lived and wrote in the nineteenth century but whose innovative contribution to the art of fiction makes it impossible to ignore them in any account of the origins of the modern novel; it also includes the so-called 'modernists' and those who in the mid- and late twentieth century have emerged as outstanding practitioners of this genre. The scope is, inevitably, international; not only, in the migratory and exile-haunted world of our century, do writers refuse to heed national frontiers – 'English' literature lays claim to Conrad the Pole, Henry James the American, and Joyce the Irishman – but geniuses such as Flaubert, Dostoevski and Kafka have had an influence on the fiction of many nations.

Each volume in the series is intended to provide an introduction to the fiction of the writer concerned, both for those approaching him or her for the first time and for those who are already familiar with some parts of the achievement in question and now wish to place it in the context of the total *oeuvre*. Although essential information relating to the writer's life and times is given, usually in an opening chapter, the approach is primarily critical and the emphasis is not upon 'background' or generalisations but upon close examination of important texts. Where an author is notably prolific, major texts have been made to convey, more summarily, a sense of the nature and quality of the author's work as a whole. Those who want to read further will find suggestions in the select bibliography included in each volume. Many novelists are, of course, not only novelists but also poets, essayists, biographers, dramatists, travel writers and so forth; many have practised shorter forms of fiction; and many have written letters or kept diaries that constitute a significant part of their literary output. A brief study cannot hope to deal with all these in detail, but where the shorter fiction and the non-fictional writings, public and private, have an important relationship to the novels, some space has been devoted to them.

NORMAN PAGE

Preface

Anthony Powell gained his reputation as a novelist more slowly than his near-contemporaries Evelyn Waugh and Graham Greene, but he is today equally regarded by many readers, and increasingly widely known, in North America and other parts of the English-speaking world as well as in Britain. Always up to date in his concern with the craft of writing, he can be thought of as classical in his humanism, and in his assumption that a novelist's first duty is to entertain. 'It's extraordinary how interesting his stuff is', P. G. Wodehouse said. Others – Kingsley Amis, Philip Larkin, Roy Fuller, Anthony Burgess – have awarded ampler praise; Wodehouse's remark recognises Powell's idiosyncratic, addictive appeal. This study aims to explore and illustrate his unusual blend of comedy, satire, poetic fantasy and the anatomising of melancholy. It covers his novels from the 1930s to the 1980s, while giving most attention to the novel-sequence that is his principal achievement.

I have followed Anthony Powell's own practice in abbreviating the sequence's full title, *A Dance to the Music of Time*, to *Dance*. Numbers in parenthesis after quotations refer to chapters or parts of novels.

N.McE

1
Fact and Fiction

There are many connections between Anthony Powell's life and his fiction. He published five novels between 1931 and 1939 and two more in the 1980s; *A Dance to the Music of Time* (1951–76) is a novel-sequence in twelve volumes.[1] His memoirs, *To Keep the Ball Rolling*, appeared in four volumes between 1976 and 1982. Powell has warned us against the idea of real models for fictional creations, but he does yield to the attraction of exploring the autobiographical sources of his novels, and readers who enjoy his books will probably share his gossipy inquisitiveness about how people, places and events can be linked with characters, settings and stories.[2] The memoirs are full of clues to starting points for the novelist's imagination – or, in his phrase, 'creative fantasy'. The relation between fact and fiction, always problematic, is most interesting in the case of Nicholas Jenkins, narrator of *Dance*, whose career and personality resemble the author's. Powell told an interviewer, 'Nick is a person like myself', and added that 'if you're writing a novel you must have a point of view, and it should be one fairly near your own'.[3] *To Keep the Ball Rolling* is useful as an introduction to the novels for what it shows of their background and of their approach to life.

One way in which Powell resembles Jenkins is in his reserve. Voluble about others, he is reticent about himself and his outlook emerges, obliquely, in the portraits of contemporaries, especially writers, which occupy far more of the memoirs than passages which simply tell about himself. *Infants of the Spring*, the first volume of memoirs, presents Powell as a boy quite unlike the young Henry Yorke (the future novelist Henry Green), a friend at preparatory school, at Eton and at Oxford. An only child, born in December 1905 (and christened Anthony Dymoke), Powell grew up supposing that he would follow his father as a regular army officer. Although his parents did not encourage him in this, he was fourteen before 'the incongruity of any such ambition dawned even on myself'. Nick Jenkins's childhood in the haunted bungalow in the first section of *The Kindly Ones* is, we are told, partially drawn from life, and the young Nick, steeped with scholarly precision in military lore, observing a tempestuous but secure home life thoughtfully, fancifully and acceptingly, is often brought to mind by Powell's hints about the sort of child he was. Yorke surprised him by ragging his father 'in a manner I should never have dreamt of using towards my own' and also by complaints about 'tensions at home'.[4] It is no surprise to readers of Powell's fiction to learn that he felt from an early age, as perhaps a soldier's son should, that the basic disposition of things is not to be questioned.

Powell enjoyed his four years at Eton (1919–23), chancing on agreeable company and a relatively civilised regime.

> I could not have been more fortunate in my Eton house. A. M. Goodhart's was not merely a 'bad' house, but universally agreed to be far the 'worst' house in the school. Its record at every branch of sport was unimaginably low; its only silver trophy, the Lower Boy Singing Cup. Tolerant scepticism was the note struck.[5]

Infants of the Spring dwells on the pleasures of the Arts Society and of drawing lessons at the Studio. Powell quotes with dry amusement from his housemaster's reports on his 'moodiness' and 'way of speaking which may give offence to some because it seems to imply a cold superiority or frame of mind too judicial'.[6] He is not inclined to comment or to make a story out of whatever lay behind these impressions. Instead he offers anecdotes about friends, including Harold Acton, Robert Byron the travel-writer – and Hubert Duggan (brother of Alfred Duggan, also at school) who contributed some traits to Stringham in *Dance*. Cyril Connolly was a slightly older contemporary whom he did not meet until Oxford. Powell's portrait of Connolly fits into this stage of *Infants of the Spring*, however, because 'A Georgian Boyhood', the last section of Connolly's *Enemies of Promise*, is the best-known account of Eton at that time. Connolly's school sketches are more dramatic and far more self-centred than Powell's. He is one of several English writers of about the same age who made what Powell calls 'myths' of their schooldays: Graham Greene, Christopher Isherwood and John Betjeman are some of the others. Connolly's Etonian myth is simple in outline: brilliantly successful at school he found adult life an anticlimax and sank into sloth and boredom. Powell praises Connolly's 'passionate interest in himself', which he says is rare and not to be confused with selfishness, the 'personal crater' being too awful for most of us to contemplate. He notes, however, that this 'gift of self-examination' was paid for by lack of interest in others.[7] Disinclined to mythologise himself, in his memoirs, Powell is always interested in the myths by which others live. It was presumably in his Eton years, while Connolly acted out his short-lived triumph, that Powell began to learn the role of the detached observer.

The Oxford of the novels is a place of 'crushing melancholy', as in the opening lines of *Books Do Furnish a Room* where Jenkins returns, twenty years on: 'before the local climate had time to impair health, academic contacts disturb the spirit, a more immanent gloom was re-established, its sinewy grip in a flash making one young again'. Powell was at Balliol College (1923–6), where he relieved his 'deep melancholy' in various ways. Reading for a degree in history, he was tutored by Kenneth Bell, Fellow of Balliol and 'rather a great man'. Bell taught that history was about people rather than theories: 'Yes, that may well be true – but we shall never know what Charles V felt like in the early morning.'[8] Powell found this approach congenial and he willingly accepted Bell's teaching of 'history for itself', not as material for obtaining a First Class degree. He did not obtain a First, but his lifelong interest in history appears in his novels. 'Rackety goings-on' occupied spare time, especially in the Hypocrites Club, where Evelyn Waugh and Alfred Duggan were also members. There were also (male) undergraduate 'salons' of the kind seen, in a temperate version, in *Dance*, at the don Sillery's tea-parties.

Some readers have identified Sillery with F. F. Urquhart, Dean of Balliol, known as 'Sligger'. *Infants of the Spring* denies any connection. An Oxford figure resembling Sillery at least in having presided over a circle of favoured undergraduates was Maurice Bowra, Fellow (later Warden) of Wadham. Originator and subject of countless Oxford stories, Bowra set out to impress, and he influenced Powell for a while. He classified those he invited to lunches and dinners in a personal set of terms: 'presentable', 'unpresentable', 'able', 'able, I'm afraid', 'upright', 'nice stupid man', 'shit of hell'.[9] Combined with a creed of intelligent selfishness and social combat, these classifications must have seemed attractively free of Victorian humbug, and Bowra's aggressive use of them probably encouraged Powell to think satirically about people as social performers. The earliest novels show his expertise in refining upon such types. Bowra is also like Sillery, however, in accepting the limits of an institution for the sake of power, and this is a type of personality which, although interesting, is always felt to be alien in the novels. In 1926, at the age of twenty, with 'a vague intention to write a novel myself one of these days', Powell was glad to leave Oxford for London.[10]

Messengers of Day, the second volume of the memoirs, begins with the finding of rooms in Shepherd Market (where Jenkins finds his too), cheap, and convenient for smart dances in Mayfair, an 'enclave' known from Michael Arlen's best-selling novel *The Green Hat* (1924). Among people encountered in the first year in London, Constant Lambert, already a composer, was exceptional: 'the first contemporary of mine [within months in age] I found, intellectually speaking, wholly sympathetic'. Conversation with Lambert offered a pleasant change from the then Oxford manner of 'treating the arts as if they were a useful social weapon'. The description of his talk as 'a barrage of ideas, jokes, fantasy, quotations, apt instances, things that had struck him as he walked through London' suggests that the freedom with which these elements mingle in *A Dance to the Music of Time* may owe something to Lambert, who died in 1951, the year in which the first volume of the sequence was published; Powell lost an ideal reader as well as a friend. For some commentators, Hugh Moreland in the novels 'is' Lambert. Powell corrects that view, but acknowledges that 'if I have been skilful enough to pass on any echo of Lambert's incomparable wit, then Moreland is like him'.[11] Being intellectually sympathetic is a criterion in all the novels; all the other characters in *Dance* might be placed at relative distances away from Moreland who is closest in this respect to the Narrator.

Powell began work for the publishing house of Duckworth's in 1926, experience reflected in *What's Become of Waring*. He helped to arrange for the firm to publish Evelyn Waugh's *Rossetti: His Life and Works* (1928), and almost arranged for them to publish *Decline and Fall* (1928), the first part of which Waugh read to him in an early draft. Waugh is the novelist with whom Powell is most often compared. They were satirists of high society, opposed to the left-wing movements of the 1930s; each wrote a trilogy about the 1939–45 war; both are craftsmen in prose style and in fictional form. Waugh's farce and caricature are so vivid that even lazy readers find them immediately entertaining; this makes his books (especially the early novels) enjoyable for a relatively wide audience, but they are also more simply conceived and more fantastical than Powell's. Noting this difference, in *Messengers of Day*, Powell says that Waugh had a genuine (and fixed) belief in simplified human types which appealed to his imagination, and that he refused to consider 'the contradictions and paradoxes' of actual experience.[12] Such complications were the interest and amusement of Powell as a party-goer and 'dancing-man' in the later 1920s; and his starting-point as a novelist.

Messengers of Day notes that Waugh regarded 'smart life' with 'a love/hate not unlike Thackeray's'.[13] Powell found smart life congenial and observed it with the sharp eye for absurdities that informs the early novels, but without either Thackeray's moral disapproval or his tendency, shared by Waugh, to glamorise the upper classes. Conventional upper-class life is counterpointed in the novels by scenes among Bohemians – writers, journalists, artists, musicians, actors, people living by creative and intellectual means, at various social levels ranging from 'smart' circles to those Thackeray names 'shabby genteel'. These two milieux reflect Powell's party-going in his early London years. Like Jenkins, he frequented dinners and balls in Mayfair and Belgravia, and also 'rackety' but not necessarily low-life goings-on in pubs and restaurants in Soho. The latter included Maxim's Chinese Restaurant in Gerard Street, which resembled Casanova's Chinese Restaurant in *Dance* and Castano's, run by an Italian in Greek Street, the prototype of Foppa's. The Ritz is still the Ritz in the novels, with a bronze nymph like the one Jenkins meditates in *The Acceptance World* – 'although stark naked, the nymph looked immensely respectable'[14] – in its palm court. Interaction between the different but overlapping social worlds represented by Belgravia and Soho presented Powell with good comic opportunities, as we see, for example, when Mr Deacon and Gypsy Jones attend Mrs Andriadis's party, in *A Buyer's Market*.

In 1934 Powell married Lady Violet Pakenham, daughter of the 5th Earl of Longford and sister of Lady Pansy, wife of the painter Henry Lamb. This is another way in which he resembles Jenkins, an only child who marries into a large and widely ramifying family. The Tollands of the novel, collectively and individually, resemble, to a certain extent, the Pakenhams. Powell seems to have played a game with such resemblances, more entertaining to his immediate circle than to the general reader. His biographer will presumably reveal more details than are to be found in the memoirs. One obvious point of comparison is in the almost complete exclusion from *Dance*, as from the memoirs, of the narrator's wife. Lady Isobel is sensible, intelligent and likes party-going as well as books. We learn little more. Some readers of the novels have felt that the autobiographical aspect of the narrator has interfered with the author's freedom to bring him to full fictional life. This is a complicated question. In his remarks on fiction Powell often endorses, in effect, a comment made by Rose Macaulay and quoted in *Messengers of Day*: dismissing as silly the question of whether a subject for a novel was interesting, she said 'subjects are entirely a matter of how they are treated by the author'.[15] Powell would maintain that he was right to exclude the subject of Jenkins's marriage because it was not one he felt able to treat.

In 1936 Powell left Duckworth's and took a job with the film-company Warner Bros, composing, like Jenkins in *At Lady Molly's*, scripts for the 'Quota' of British films required by law to keep Hollywood in check. This phase in his life is related in the third volume of the memoirs, *Faces in My Time*, where the post is said to have been humble but very well paid at fifteen pounds a week. The lure of high pay took the Powells to Hollywood in the following year. He failed to find employment there, or raw material for fiction. The film episodes in *Agents and Patients* were based on memories of a German film-set visited in 1932. The trip to California was not wasted, however, because Powell got to know Scott Fitzgerald. His comments reflect what they found in common: interest in 'Dukes', Fitzgerald's term for aristocracy, and 'a writer's love for categorising people'. Seeing James Stewart sitting nearby, Fitzgerald 'watched with the fascination of one Princeton man examining another'.[16] 'Examining' is the right word for Powell's own exacting scrutiny of dress, expression and mannerisms, no detail too small to be of interest when a social species has been identified. Intelligent people in the novels share this fascination. Lord Huntercombe, in *Casanova's Chinese Restaurant*, asks after the head of the Tolland family: 'He spoke with that note almost of yearning in his voice, which peers are inclined to employ when speaking of other peers, especially of those younger than themselves of whom they disapprove.'[17] Scott Fitzgerald would have liked that precise categorisation, characteristic of Powell.

Belonging to the Emergency Reserve, Powell became an officer in the Welch Regiment in December 1939. It had been his father's regiment, and, he notes in the last volume of the memoirs, *The Strangers All Are Gone*, Ford Madox Ford's. Literary aspects of the army and military aspects of literature are special interests in Powell; his published essays include 'Proust as a Soldier'.[18] There is often comic interplay in the novels between these points of view, as in the scene in *The Soldier's Art* where General Liddament and Lieutenant Jenkins disagree about Trollope, Jenkins fearing he may be placed under arrest. 'Military mystique' has had a strong appeal throughout his life. He quotes with satisfaction C. P. Snow's remark that their hosts at a conference in Sofia could not decide whether Powell looked like a soldier or a professor.[19] He is very modest about his soldierly capacity, listing but not claiming the virtues of a company commander, and summarising them as 'almost every good quality a man can possess'. Civilians, he adds, tend to disregard the requirements of the soldier's art.[20] *Dance* depicts many unattractive military types, but the overwhelming impression throughout the sequence is of respect for a high calling. Powell's service, in Northern Ireland, and, from 1941, in Military Intelligence (Liaison), where Jenkins also finds himself, ended in an appointment with the rank of major. *Faces in My Time* makes clear how demanding, as well as enjoyable, he found wartime duties.

George Orwell's place in the memoirs comes in the first volume because he was a contemporary at school, but Powell did not come to know him well until the 1940s. They differed radically in political and social outlook. It seems likely that memories of Orwell were in mind when Erridge, the 'red Earl' of *Dance*, was sent to do 'social research' among the lower classes, and possible that Orwell's socialist views contributed to those of Erridge, derided as all such leftism is in the novels. But Powell's account of Orwell looks for points in common, and finds a touch of dandyism, reassuring to him in so startlingly different an Etonian. It includes the story of the straps under the shoes. Dining at the Café Royal in dress uniform when they met, Powell feared

Orwellian disapproval, but found that the former Burmese policeman shared his satisfaction in the straps, which, Orwell said, 'give you a feeling like nothing else in life'.[21] Orwell was perhaps in flight from everything Eton stood for, except the 'sceptical tolerance' which Powell had liked best in those he knew at school. Two themes are worth noting in the character-sketch: that political differences need not interfere with friendship or with literary appreciation; and that even the most earnest political convictions need not tyrannise a civilised mind. In the last respect the Orwell of Powell's portrait is quite unlike Erridge and the other (in his terms, uncivilised) left-wingers in *Dance*.

Likes and dislikes in reading are often mentioned in the memoirs, as an unpredictable, possibly revealing facet of character; Powell likes Kipling, for example, while Henry Yorke who expressed Kiplingesque views did not. Powell's reading has been even more extensive than Nicholas Jenkins's, although few will know all the books Nick quotes and broods about. *Messengers of Day* mentions novels which impressed and influenced him. Among old novelists, he admired Henry James and Joseph Conrad, both technically adventurous and artistically committed enough to seem modern, in contrast to Victorians such as Dickens and Trollope. E. E. Cummings's novel *The Enormous Room* (1922) made much conventional Edwardian fiction seem out of date. Hemingway's new treatment of dialogue seemed matched by that of Ronald Firbank. *Ulysses*, smuggled and read in its ninth printing (1927), was less attractive than Wyndham Lewis whose *Tarr* (1918, revised 1928) was also impressively new in method. These writers persuaded him, and most young people interested in literature in the 1920s, that a decisive break had been effected with many of the procedures of nineteenth-century English fiction: overcomplicated plots, pedestrian chronicling of events and description of settings, and overt moralising of a kind acceptable to suburban, church-going readers were all to be things of the past. Such thoughts made French literature especially exciting. It was at Oxford that Powell first read Proust's *A la recherche du temps perdu*. Flaubert and Stendhal were also read early; Balzac in middle age. Lermontov's *A Hero of Our Time*, not enjoyed at first, came to be highly regarded. It may be a clue to the difference between prewar and postwar Powell that Dostoevsky, now regarded as 'top of the league' – not only the Russian one – did not make an impact until the 1950s. (He described himself to an interviewer as surprising people in trains by laughing aloud over *The Idiot.*) But Petronius, whose *Satyricon* he read in a seventeenth-century translation, was 'probably the last writer to help form a taste still open to development'.[22]

The variety of these authors, and the comments, show the place subject-matter has in Powell's interest: the planning and the writing come first. He is, none the less, a humanist as well as a formalist and stylist, in reading tastes and in his own novels. His belief that human nature remains the same, whether observed by Petronius in the first century or by Dostoevsky in the nineteenth, might be called classical. It is not the sort of classicism which holds that everything has been said already, however, since Powell finds human nature and behaviour infinitely fascinating. He puts it in milder terms; like Nick Jenkins, he is 'interested in the details of others' lives'.[23] It has often been remarked that *Dance* can be compared to literary art of a high order but also has affinities with gossip. Nick Jenkins is a gossip of genius. John Aubrey (1626–97), biographer and antiquary, one of the great gossips of past literature, is a writer Powell liked from student days. In 1945 he returned to Oxford to work on Aubrey's manuscripts in the Bodleian library, later publishing *John Aubrey and His Friends* (1948) and an edition, *Brief Lives and Other Selected Writings of John Aubrey* (1949). The seventeenth century is a favourite period, reflected from the title *Afternoon Men* (from Robert Burton) onwards, but the reason why Aubrey is especially congenial is contained in Powell's comment on his originality: 'a new sort of sensibility is apparent, the appreciation of the oddness of the individual human being'.[24]

Powell was literary editor of *Punch* from 1953 until 1959, appointed by its then editor Malcolm Muggeridge. His sketch of Muggeridge shows his detachment from all forms of enthusiasm. This can be valuable to a comic writer. Powell is entertaining about the three separate personalities conflicting in his subject: First Muggeridge, a sceptical wit who 'treated life as a jest'; Second Muggeridge, full of 'violent political and moral animosities'; Third Muggeridge, long concealed or obscured, finally revealed 'at full strength, hot-gospelling, near messianic'. First Muggeridge suffered in this company, ending 'now so to speak a thief crucified between two Christs'.[25] Powell is equally amused by the thought of Graham Greene, in this respect his opposite as a passionate believer in commitment, as a film reviewer 'calling ... fire down from heaven – and up from hell – on the cinema and all its works'.[26] Does Powell treat life as a jest? He is neither cynical nor sentimental. His fiction implies a humanist belief in the art of living, disciplined and relaxed, sustained by the arts and by humour, tolerantly sceptical about ultimate questions. There are places, however, where he finds the human disposition to believe amusing in itself, and where some generally sympathetic readers are disturbed by the degree of detachment in his humour.

Ivy Compton-Burnett is judged, in *The Strangers All Are Gone*, to be 'one of the most gifted novelists of her generation'. Powell likes her 'severity': her power to treat the passions, including adultery, incest and homosexuality, 'in the relentless terms of Greek tragedy', while preserving 'the muted terms' of the late Victorian period in which her novels are set. He met Miss Compton-Burnett several times and liked her; she was his senior by two decades (1884–1969), but he felt that she belonged to an earlier world, 'another civilisation than one's own'.[27] Siegfried Sassoon (1886–1967), a neighbour in Somerset after the war, also seemed to be living in the past. Powell belonged to the generation, including Waugh and Greene, who felt themselves sharply different from their immediate predecessors who had grown up before the 1914–18 war. They were more emancipated in being able to take for granted the openness with which they discussed things, the passions especially, as Virginia Woolf and her circle were not. Powell treats adultery, homosexuality and other passions, including necrophilia, with a freedom from any trace of Victorian prudishness or of Bloomsbury's self-consciousness. Powell may have benefited from Ivy Compton-Burnett, none the less, in observing how artistically apt 'muted terms' can be. The earlier volumes of *Dance* contain characters, including Mr Deacon, Max Pilgrim and Heather Hopkins, Norman Chandler and Hugo Tolland, whose homosexuality is effectively presented without ever being mentioned.

Powell objects strongly to 'half-baked critics' who misread because they see a work of literature primarily as a social act. 'One of the basic human rights is to make fun of other people whoever they are.' This is declared in support of Kingsley Amis, one of the novelists recommended in *The Strangers All Are Gone*. A reviewer thought the lecherous character Evans in Amis's verse a sign of the poet's hatred of the people of South Wales; Amis happens to like people from South Wales. Since every fool and knave belongs to some respectable community or group, such muddled thinking nowadays poses a threat to the right to make fun. Another mistake of the same kind comes from regarding a novel's point of view as an end rather than a means. Many readers of *Lucky Jim* saw it as an attack on cultural values or as a novel of protest. Powell found it 'very funny' and beautifully written. He 'hardly noticed' the 'abrasive overtones apart from their being the angle from which the narrative was launched'.[28] It is narrated by an acutely disgruntled character because that is what the novel needs. Powell does not apply these points to criticism of his own work, but it is obvious how he would reply to complaints that he attacks homosexuality when he makes fun of Mr Deacon or Heather Hopkins. Powell's enlightened attitude to homosexuality can be seen throughout his memoirs. Jenkins in *Dance* is amused by sexual (and every other kind of) unorthodoxy; his ultra-conventional, and in the early volumes innocent, outlook, is the angle from which Powell launched his comedy.

Robert Nye's *Guardian* review of *Hearing Secret Harmonies* paid Powell a tribute from a different political position as 'a great artist of the right'.[29] Powell might affect surprise at the last phrase, but would hardly feel it. He would say that Jenkins's political conservatism is another aspect of 'the angle' from which the sequence is narrated, irrelevant to its quality. There is a note of satisfaction, none the less, when he remarks on the disappointment of those who welcomed Amis in the 1950s as a champion of the left.[30] Discussing the novels of V. S. Naipaul, he mentions the light touch in writing, and comedy mixed with melancholy as, perhaps, 'a true gift for comedy'. He also speaks of Naipaul's 'excoriation' of 'a world still partly bemused by 19th century sentimentalities and optimisms, to which it has added some of its own yet more futile'.[31] This is a rare open statement of political opinion, presumably felt due in loyalty to Naipaul, a friend whom he admires for courageous objectivity. Political distaste is usually implicit in the memoirs and novels.

These impressions might be organised into a 'personal myth' by C. P. Snow's observation that Powell could be taken for a soldier or a professor. He is, perhaps 'a military philosopher'. Conservatism in temperament and outlook, satisfaction in the family tradition of military service, expectation when a boy that he would be a soldier, and as a young man frequenting deb-dances and house-parties where it was common to spend at least a few years as an officer in a smart regiment, all suggest the career he might have followed, as do his terms of approval, 'smart' and 'stylish'. The army may appeal to his liking for order, but also to 'the writer's love for categorising people', noticed in Scott Fitzgerald, because regiments and ranks offer such scope for it. There also seems to be a romantic element in the 'military' side of his imagination, while he is highly disciplined as an intellectual. The pleasure in the visual arts, especially painting and architecture, apparent in the novels, has been trained by an academic interest; the Tiepolo, for example, invented for a Venetian ceiling in *Temporary Kings* is lectured about by Dr Emily Brightman, a highly disciplined don. The novels also expect us to follow attentively thoughts about a wide range of history and literature. A minor pleasure of the sequence is the brilliance of the burlesques of past styles of writing and speech. Mysticism and magic, providing many incidents and images in *Dance*, is an interest of Jenkins's; but like one of the sequence's mages, Paul Fenneau (in the first and last volumes), he is at home at 'the scholarly end' of magic.[32] Above all, writing is a strict discipline, reflected in Jenkins's 'hard cold-blooded, almost mathematical pleasure in writing and painting'.[33] The bad novelist in *Dance*, St John Clarke, is slack. Discipline of this kind unites Powell with others, including Naipaul and Amis, for whom writing is a vocation to be treated with respect.

People in the novels differ in a way which cuts across the military/intellectual division. Men and women of action who live by the will, seeking power, are contrasted with thoughtful, pleasure-seeking observers of life. Widmerpool is the extreme and most disagreeable instance of a man of the will in pursuit of power; other wilful characters are merely mischievous like Sillery; some, such as General Conyers, combine will-power with civilised qualities and they are impressive. Jenkins and Moreland are among the observers of life. Powell sympathises with the observers. His treatment of Field-Marshal Sir Bernard Montgomery is interesting, therefore, as a supreme example of a soldier of will-power. 'The Field-Marshal' in *The Military Philosophers* closely resembles Montgomery, about whom Powell writes rather dryly in *Faces in My Time*: not successful in 'military chic', and likely 'to inspire confidence rather than admiration or devotion'.[34] Jenkins has more to say.

> The eyes were deep set and icy cold. You thought at once of an animal, though a creature not at all in the stylised manner of the two colonels at my Divisional Headquarters, reminiscent respectively of the dog-faced and bird-faced Egyptian deities. No such artificial formality shaped these features, and to say, for example, they resembled those of a fox or ferret would be to imply a disparagement not at all sought. Did the features, in fact, suggest some mythical beast, say one of those encountered in *Alice in Wonderland*, full of awkward questions and downright statements? This sense, that here was perhaps a personage from an imaginary world, was oddly sustained by the voice. It was essentially an army voice, but precise, controlled, almost mincing, when not uttering some awful warning, as to Gauthier de Graef. There was a faint and faraway reminder of the clergy, too; parsonic, yet not in the least numinous, the tone of the incumbent ruthlessly dedicated to his parish, rather than the hierophant celebrating divine mysteries. At the same time, one guessed this parish priest regarded himself as in a high class of hierophancy too, whatever others might think.[35]

The first impression is of questing aggression, or tactical flight, in 'fox or ferret', in spite of the Narrator's demur. The talkative beasts of *Alice* are aptly funny, given that we are bound by the context of the novel to think of Montgomery, even if we only know him from pictures and recordings; these are authoritative creatures. The image of the parson emphasises the disciplined vocation of the setting of so much ruthlessness and self-regard. All the images convey will-power as an alien, mysterious force, animal, mythical or priestly. The last phrase insists more effectively on the strength of the determination because it does not refer directly to the Field-Marshal but to the parish priest brought to mind by a hint in the voice, something faint and faraway but definitely there. Jenkins is putting into words not the man but his daemon or charisma.

Jenkins tells us that the Field-Marshal lacks 'elegance', and goes on to reflect that 'will-power exercised unrelentingly over a lifetime – as opposed to its display in brilliant flashes – is apt on the whole to be the enemy of elegance'.[36] He has in mind the failure of experiments in adapting uniform, matching those of Montgomery, but he thinks of a possible connection with moral elegance, since both are absent in Hitler and Mussolini, and indeed in many of the great commanders of the past, with Wellington perhaps as an exception. Jenkins does not care for the Field-Marshal, although he acknowledges that the man's efficiency is what modern war requires. Officers he admires have known the 'secret' of 'a lounging smartness'; for him such outward signs are very telling.

Will-power versus elegance is a workable principle for ordering a discussion of the books. There are, of course, many others. Powell wishes his readers to be sceptical about the value of such schemes. He has condemned one approach, denying that his fiction is 'about' the decline or decay or civilisation.[37] Otherwise he is interested in 'the consumer end of the Arts, what the reader inevitably adds . . . not necessarily in an uncreative manner'.[38] He would agree, furthermore, with Jenkins's dictum, in *The Soldier's Art*, that 'to think one thing at one moment, another at the next, is the prescriptive right of every human being'.[39] Portraits in the memoirs are written in the awareness of how unknowable other people are, and the novels make a comic art out of uncertainty about what characters are like, how variously they can be discussed, imagined, told stories about. Doubt is an essential ingredient, both comic and sad, in Powell's narratives. The will is sensed or elegance observed, but the oddness of individuals escapes definition. People offer endless scope for theorising, and for story-telling.

'Myth' is a favourite term, in Powell, for story-telling. It has the sense of 'falsehood' when it applies to wilful characters who invent roles, or 'myths', to sustain their egotism. It is also, more often and more interestingly, a term for 'creative fantasy', the means whereby the raw material of life develops into literature. The 'magician' Aleister Crowley, perhaps the most unpleasant individual portrayed in the memoirs, illustrates both these concepts of myth. He is seen as a power-seeker ensnared in a crude myth of his own invention. As 'the Beast 666', Crowley figures in *Messengers of Day*, and in the accounts of many others who knew him, as a pitiable and sinister personality. In many superficial respects, Crowley resembles Doctor Trelawney in *Dance*. Crowley's ritual greeting and the required response were only slightly less ridiculous than those Powell invented for his character.[40] But Trelawney is a richly independent comic creation. In his speech, which parodies the most high-mystical jargon of the age of Madame Blavatsky, in his costumes and paraphernalia, his dealings with other mages, his place in Jenkins's memory and epic fights of fancy, he grows into a figure of 'myth' in the best sense of this complex word; and it is in this respect rather than in any connections with a real-life counterpart, that he is typical of Powell. He takes so strong a hold on the imagination that he seems true to life.

2

Novels of the 1930s

Afternoon Men's original jacket, designed by Misha Black from an idea put to him by the author (who controlled the book's production at Duckworth's), shows a wooden-jointed lay-figure, a puppet-like painter's model, tipsily posed swaying and mishandling a wineglass, photographed close-up against a plain background. This bare, stylised image, the first impression for the earlier readers of Powell's first novel, in 1931, implied an up-to-date work far-removed from loose, baggy novels of a conventional, old-fashioned sort. A second impression came from the headings of the three sections, 'Montage', 'Perihelion', 'Palindrome', which can be interpreted in various ways.[41] They seem intended as signals that intelligent attention is expected; reminders, in Powell's words from another context, that works of art require creative effort from the consumer.[42] Reading confirms these impressions because *Afternoon Men*, more emphatically than the next four novels, proclaims itself avant-garde. More than half the text is dialogue, much of it curt and informal in the manner made fashionable by Hemingway. There is relatively little guidance in the delineation of characters, discussion of themes, or telling of the tale. Characters, themes and plot, indeed, are minimal. The story develops in a succession of scenes which seem casual and random. Some chapters occupy less than a page. Yet we are conscious of design on the part of the novelist as editor, cutting and shaping material. A third feature of the novel's presentation, however, which offers a guide to reading, is an epigraph traditional in source and straightforward in its bearing. It is from Robert Burton's *The Anatomy of Melancholy* (1621):

> as if they had heard that enchanted horn of Astolpho, that English duke in Ariosto, which never sounded but all his auditors were mad, and for fear ready to make away with themselves

... they are a company of giddy-heads, afternoon men.

The title is neatly re-applied to the haunters of cocktail-bars in modern London, Bohemians giddy-headed from party-going and from free thinking and free love. Memories of Burton's massive, erudite compendium make a pleasing background to Powell's lightness of touch and to the intellectual vacuity of the social world he portrays, in the speculations of a young journalist, for example, in Chapter 6: 'I'm not a religious chap. I don't know anything about that sort of thing. But there must be something beyond all this sex-business.' Such a contrast can be regarded as modernist. There is also a suggestion of Powell's classical, humanist cast of mind in the way that, on a scale much smaller than Burton's but with as intimate a feel for melancholy, *Afternoon Men* shows how the vapours and humours of the present day goad men to giddyness and fear, madness and suicide, as they have done in every age.

Melancholy is always close to comedy in Powell. Trivial things which reflect the messiness and the flatness of everyday life are humorously brought out all through the novel by a technique of slow motion. One example is the treatment of the opening of a bottle of wine in Chapter 9: 'Lola said: "Gwen will open it. She opens them very well." Gwen screwed it well down into the cork and pulled. Nearly all of the cork came out at last and Gwen went out to fetch some glasses.' There has already been an argument about who should do the opening. A page later, after the drink has been strained through a handkerchief to remove the cork, the characters are still discussing the mishap. Everyone agrees that Gwen draws corks very well, 'as well as any man'. Some men have no skill. Their corks go into the wine. Atwater, the novel's foremost character, admits that this almost always happens to him. Gwen does not often break the cork. One good result of this slowing down of the writing to the pace of such incidents appears in observations such as 'Nearly all of the cork came out at last', where timing adds to the amusement of the plain exact wording. This was the beginning of an unhurried comedy to be developed to its heights in *A Dance to the Music of Time*. Another result is the wringing of comedy from very flat, commonplace talk, presented with painstaking completeness and without comment, another early stage in the growth of Powell's laconic art.

Control of the writing makes a comment on the mess of 'Nearly all of the cork came out at last', and in many other quietly mocking sentences. Exact reporting of grotesque behaviour, during the parties that occupy much of the book, benefits from calm rhythm and neutral tone: 'Barlow's brother was wandering about finishing up several drinks that had been abandoned by their owners' (3). Ugliness, especially in faces in the streets or in public places, arouses a pungency, however, which seems less artful than writing where disapproval is implicit: the doorman at a gallery in Chapter 12 is 'an ape-faced dotard' and 'a senile cretin', and other figures are declared repulsive in this way. Disappointing physical features are more wittily conveyed elsewhere, for example in the case of Gwen, 'of whom Undershaft had once said that she looked the sort of boy who might win a scholarship in chemistry' (9). Grotesque appearance can also be purely funny: '"I often think of the masters at school," he said. "Men who could have made fortunes merely by walking across a music-hall stage preferred to teach little boys mathematics"' (23). 'Merely' adds the needed touch of fantasy. Such open exuberance is less characteristic than subdued amusement, in deftly worded observation of all ungraceful, unskilled, inelegant phenomena.

Dialogue often seems notable for banality. A girl spills beer on a man's legs in Chapter 2.

> The girl sat on the sofa next to Atwater. She said:
> 'Is your friend angry?'
> 'Yes.'
> 'I was looking for my bag.'
> 'Were you?'
> 'It was suddenly knocked out of my hand and all over him.'
> 'He's very wet.'
> 'I expect he'll be able to dry himself somehow.'
> 'There must be a way.'
> 'Will you get me another drink,' she said.
> 'What?'
> 'Anything.'

Naturalistic and lifelike, this has been carefully contrived and is as mannered as any artificial social comedy. The girl's unconcern sounds voluble given Atwater's restraint, which all but conceals his hints at her fault. 'Were you?' and 'There must be some way' are examples of how dialogue is slowed into comedy; his judicious caution, in these remarks, emphasises her casual, 'Anything'. There are many examples of Powell's good ear for how haphazardly people speak: 'Of course, the only time that I really use candles is when my lights fuse, which is quite often' (9). This may have been one of the overheard remarks Powell says he jotted down while preparing *Afternoon Men*. If so, his craft has found an entertaining context for it – out of the unnaturalistic tides of actual dull talk. The effects of drink on speech, in this novel, make another preliminary study to be developed in later books. Drink's pomposity is caught in comparison with a more dignified style and theme: 'The young man leant across the bar, and said: "I'll tell you this, George. I was squiffy after two of them. It's a fact." He said it confidentially, as one might say: "The gift of tongues descended on me last night after months of fasting"' (14). The long speech made by Fotheringham in Chapter 6 illustrates the fluent waywardness and bogus rhetoric of a chronic drunk at a certain level of intoxication, but is more attractively composed and consistently funny than one would find in life. Such passages show the start of a skill with drunken English that matured in the Dionysian scenes of *Dance*.

Messiness and flatness are usually found in trivial pursuits in *Afternoon Men*, but its best sequence concerns the attempted suicide of Atwater's friend, the painter Pringle, a sad though preposterous victim of Astolpho's horn. The novel's cast assemble at Pringle's seaside cottage in Part III; when another painter takes his mistress, he decides to drown himself, and leaves a note of explanation on top of the cold beef in the dining-room. When the others find it they sit down, dispirited, to eat the beef. Powell's gift for ludicrous aspects of odd social occasions begins to appear. '"May I have the beetroot, Sophy?" said Mrs Race. She looked straight ahead of her. They ate in silence' (28). Embarrassment is treated as a stronger force than anything else that might be involved in self-slaughter, here and in the following pages. The idea that the tipping of the fisherman who pulled Pringle out of the sea would present the greatest difficulty arising from the suicide bid is explored with a thoroughness characteristic of Powell's later comedy. After lunch Pringle's guests collect his clothes from the beach: 'Everybody took a garment'. When he reappears, some hours later, his friends now accustomed to his suicide, he is full not of remorse but of complaints: people took no notice of him, when he had decided to be rescued, except for one man who threatened to report him to the police for bathing without a costume. A fisherman duly arrives to reclaim the clothes loaned to Pringle, and the question of what 'the man' ought to be paid overwhelms any conceivable concern for Pringle's presumed despair: 'I'm not sure that seven and six is really enough' (30). Discussion advances the tip to a pound. Powell yields to facetiousness only once, allowing Mrs Race to say that a pound would be a bad precedent, given that Pringle will return to the cottage later: 'It may happen again'. This apart, his characters earnestly and plausibly cavill over the price before deciding to wake the convalescent Pringle, who protests, 'But, I mean, a pound is enormous'. Straws are thoughtfully split. Two men were in the boat but only one did the job of pulling Pringle out. Fifteen shillings is eventually handed over, for which the fisherman says, 'Ta'. Pringle notes with satisfaction, 'That was obviously the right sum'. He is less than happy. One of his guests, overexcited by the suicide, has spilt medicine on a valuable rug; olive oil has got into the works of his wristwatch during his time away. Jealousy, despair, death, are diminished by such little preoccupations, and tragedy succumbs to social worries under the inspection of a style which was to grow more sure of itself, but is already recognisably Powellian.

Another species of melancholy anatomised in *Afternoon Men* and in all the early works is irritation. During Atwater's morning, in Chapter 5, at the museum where he 'guards some of the national collection', his hangover from the previous party is aggravated by assaults from three experts in causing mental torment on a small scale. The messenger-boy who chews gum is the least of these. The archaeologist Nosworth chooses Atwater's desk to write notes at while talking aloud about the history of the pains in his back. Dr Crouch, a member of the public who insists on an interview, is a more difficult case.

> Atwater wondered how long he was going on and whether he was a lunatic or some semi-serious nuisance and work-creator. He did not listen. He knew that the best he could hope for was that he should avoid hearing it all more than once.

The phrasing suggests that Kingsley Amis, also a specialist in irritability, is indebted to the style of early Powell. 'Semi-serious nuisance and work-creator' has an academic air of precision in classifying a particular sort of social menace which today sounds Amisian, and so does Atwater's calculating, while trying to shield his mind from it, of the extent of unavoidable boredom. Atwater escapes from Crouch, but only temporarily; he has carelessly left Crouch's pamphlet on the unification of craniometric and cephalometric calculations in the keeping of Nosworth, who is translating Danish verse. Nosworth demands to be given 'an attribute of the sea' other than *wine-dark*. By the time the pamphlet has been extracted from Nosworth's note-case, Dr Crouch has sealed his victory, by leaving with a promise to return.

> The boy went away. Nosworth came into the room. He said:
> 'What day of the week is it?'
> 'Saturday.'
> 'Oh, is it?'
> 'I think so.'
> The morning passed slowly.

'Life is very long', laments T. S. Eliot in 'The Hollow Men' (1925). That ennui, often voiced in the literature of the interwar period, is well observed in *Afternoon Men*, which reminds us of what it is like to suffer, while amusing us by contemplating the condition.

Messengers of Day says that Powell was surprised by reviewers of *Afternoon Men* who 'treated as a savage attack on contemporary habits what had seemed to me something of an urban pastoral (if that is a permissible concept) depicting the theme of unavailing love'. Atwater loves the beautiful Susan Nunnery, who thinks that love is 'a bore', evades his loving pursuit, and runs away at the end of the novel with a richer man who takes her to New York. Atwater is not too absorbed in love to allow himself other affairs, however; he seduces the model Lola, although lovelessly and, it seems, without pleasure; and in the same gloomy spirit he makes love with Pringle's mistress while Pringle is swimming out to his intended drowning. Casual sex, like reckless drinking, is regarded not with a moralist's disapproval but with a novelist's interest in its melancholy: its flat, messy irritations. Unavailing love is another form of melancholy, but one which sends Atwater on the last page back to a new party of the sort he was approaching in the first pages, in a sad cycle, or 'palindrome'.

He and the indolent, hedonistic shepherds and nymphs of the London of cocktail parties are shown with a refusal to be solemn, let alone angry, which justifies Powell's complaint about reviewers who spoke of 'savage attack'. It is understandable, however, that early readers should have found it hard to sight the author's point of view, because this first novel experiments with a concealment of intent which is characteristic of all Powell's fiction. Distance is his aim. The *Times Literary Supplement* reviewer of 1931 remarked on 'ironic precision' in reproducing talk, and ended by praising 'a humorous veracity of observation'. The last phrase is especially apt, except that it applies equally well to Jane Austen. Powell, as some critics have said, may be thought to belong to the tradition in which she wrote – both being sharp observers of English manners. She offers a useful contrast in one respect, however; her authorial presence, laughing at fools, stricturing knaves, is so immediate and so unlike Powell's inscrutability.

> Atwater read the copy of *Vogue*, including the advertisements for removing hair, as he now knew nearly all the rest of it by heart and it was too early in the morning to go on with *Urn Burial*.

This implies no attack against *Vogue*, or Atwater, or the hollowness of alienated modern civilisation. It is a rueful reflection, typical of Powell, on the ups and downs of one's reading, the humour of linking hair-removal advertisements with Sir Thomas Browne all but suppressed, so that the reader looks at the amusement rather than joining in. That detachment is present in many of the funniest passages of *Afternoon Men*, and throughout the next four novels.

Venusberg (1932) is the story of a young English journalist's visit, for his newspaper, to a Baltic country. Like *Afternoon Men*, it relates gloomy love-affairs. There is less dialogue and more of a story, although nobody would read it for the interest of what happens next. Lushington's detached, sensitive, polite, ironic observations are the sources of amusement in this very funny novel; it is possible to see Lushington as a prototype of Nicholas Jenkins. The people about him, two contrasted Counts, his mistress Ortrud Mavrin and his old schoolfriend Da Costa, honorary attaché at the British legation, among others, engage in 'rackety goings on' like those of the first novel, rendered as before in mockingly meticulous prose. This time death interrupts the parties, for the city of *Venusberg* is on the edge of Soviet Russia, and bedevilled by political fanatics. These do not appear, but Da Costa and Ortrud are accidentally shot and killed, going home from the annual ball given by the nobility, in the course of an attempt by some of the fanatics to assassinate the chief of police.

This novel shows advances in the art of creating comedy out of absurd situations. Pringle's attempt at suicide was the first fully successful instance in Powell's work of an anecdote explored with loving care for its comic possibilities. In *Venusberg* there are more examples of this through exploring. Powell plans and relates stories so effectively that, even when they seem to have been composed from very conventional elements of popular humour, the writing freshens them into life. A good example is the scene in which, in Chapter 17, Professor Mavrin visits the restaurant where his wife is lunching with her lover.

Lushington has met and started an affair with the beautiful Ortrud Mavrin on the boat journey to the Baltic city in which most of the novel takes place. Although its polite social life, amid diplomatic, military, academic and shabbily aristocratic circles, is close and given to gossip, her husband is easily deceived and kept out of the way. When Lushington and a crony visit the Mavrins's flat, the Professor appears in his dressing-gown and is sent away to make himself presentable; by the time he reappears, in full evening-dress, his guests are departing. This prepares us for the scene in which Lushington and Ortrud lunch together at a restaurant where the Professor never goes. When he does turn up one day, he sits at the next table without noticing them. Ortrud has to catch his attention. Mavrin is delighted by this happy chance: 'he was in splendid form . . . and questioned Lushington about the history of the sonnet sequence in English literature'. Had the novel been filmed (as some hints in its text suggest Powell may have hoped) this would probably have been treated as a familiar kind of farcical scene arousing laughter at the short-sighted and duped professor. It is essential to the fun Powell has with his scene that there should be no open reference to the adultery, no flicker of crude, farcical amusement at the expense of the learned cuckold. The amusement is all in the telling. It begins with the naturalising of a scene which resembles farce, prompting thoughts about how farce does appear in life. Mavrin is formal, for example – 'Too kind, too kind' – but not in an artificial manner intended to add to his absurdity, as farce would require. Instead his slightly stilted, educated foreigner's English is appropriately courteous. The phrase 'in splendid form', emphasising the excellence of his talk, more impressive, it is explained, because outside his field, develops the balance in the comedy between the breadth of his intellectual range and the one point that he overlooks. His topic is just right. A scholar in the continental tradition might well choose English sonnet sequences for lunchtime conversation. Without being absurdly abstruse, it is likely to test Lushington's resources – a punishment, perhaps. Powell is often amused by the ways in which theorising can interfere with or supplant personal matters, the pressure of thought so urgent that everything else is overlooked or forgotten. There is a lively comic interplay between absurd and dignified, artificial and naturalistic, cerebral and passionate aspects of the situation, which the precisely worded, quietly cadenced writing exploits: 'it was one of the Professor's outstanding merits that he rarely spoke of his own subject, psychology'.

This last touch is developed later into a part of the novel's ironic scheme. Professor Mavrin does condescend to speak of his own subject in Chapter 28, where he lectures Lushington on 'the dark and secret places' which lurk 'in the realm of the subconscious'. He is suspicious about his wife, whose behaviour suggests that she is in love with another man. Such are the strange workings of the subconscious, he maintains, that she appears to be jealous of Lushington's friendship with Da Costa, with whom she is obviously in love. Lushington pleads that psychology is too 'morbid' a subject to talk about on a lovely day. Actually, Da Costa, although heterosexual by inclination, finds women so boring that he avoids them whenever possible. Lushington's girl-friend in England, who loves Da Costa, knows this but cannot quite believe it. She thinks him, rather than Lushington, Ortrud's lover when she hears at the end that they were killed together during the attack on the chief of police, a chance association which the Professor will also misinterpret. Almost all the circumstances of the novel are ironic in one way or another. Da Costa is shot just when he has decided to abandon the diplomatic service and go to Crete as an archaeologist. His death removes Lushington's rival for the girl in London at the same time as it removes her rival for his love.

Some ironies are subtler than these. When 'Count' Bobel, a character of boundless and exuberant vulgarity who has been a nuisance since they met on the boat, appears in his hotel sitting-room moments before the Bellamys from the British legation are due to arrive, Lushington pretends that he has a girl in his bed-room. Bobel explodes with laughter. He explains the situation to his ladies: 'They agreed with the Count that it was a good joke'. Their laughter continues for some time. Powell often uses such non-jokes as weapons against the humourless characters who enjoy them. In this case, however, where fastidious Lush-ington seems to triumph over coarse Bobel, there is a further twist in store. The ruse succeeds in dislodging Bobel, who leaves laughing almost too much for words. The Count would never understand Lushington's motive, or why the Bellamys, who see Bobel in the passage, think him socially 'very impossible' (26). These are the sorts of incongruity by which Lushington, like the novelist, is quietly amused. On the boat home, however, he finds that Bobel has arranged for them to share a cabin.

One of the themes Professor Mavrin looks forward to discussing with Lushington, at 'a time when we have many hours before us', is 'Thomas Hardy and his belief in the inevitability of circum-stances' (15). Bobel's presence in the cabin is inevitable because this is how literature brings in its revenges. There are suggestions in *Venusberg* that Powell shares something of Hardy's belief about inevitability in life. There is a genuine Count on the boat out from England, who cuts the ace of spades when the fortune-telling Baroness Puckler offers her 'special pack'. Count Scherbatcheff assumes at once that the card of death foretells his grandmother's demise, not entirely a matter for regret: 'In England you do not make scenes. But my grandmother does not try to control herself. She screams. She throws herself on the floor' (11). It is Scherbat-cheff who dies, in Chapter 27, and the un-English grandmother invites Lushington to his funeral. There are various other little ironies making patterns in life, foreshadowing the bolder use of magic and coincidence (or what seems to be coincidence) in *Dance*. Hardy's hammer-blows of fate represent a far extreme, however, from the delicacy and tact of Powell's contriving.

He is delicate and elusive, too, in his treatment of modern history. The city, never named in the text, nicknamed by the title, belongs to a new republic created in the aftermath of the

Russian Revolution, as was Estonia, which Powell had visited briefly during a longer stay in Finland, a country that also contributed background to *Venusberg*. Although his aim here, as in all his work, is to entertain, Powell takes care to be accurate in recording the prejudices and social divisions of these Baltic societies: Russians are socially ostracised by patriots, including the highly civilised Professor Mavrin. Many have been uprooted and impoverished by the Revolution, or, like Bobel, pretend to have been. Any generally accepted notion about the modern age tends to be gently undermined, as in the later novels. The poverty of Count Scherbatcheff's family is rather movingly shown, but the idea that such a man would be obsessed with regret for the past is contradicted by many of his remarks. 'At least we have comfortable quarters. *Enfin*, it is not the Scherbatcheff Palace in Petersburg, but that house was more draughty than any other that I have known and its rooms were for ever full of relations whom I disliked' (19). The idea that the sexual freedom taken for granted by many of the characters is a feature of a new, shaken but emancipated society is also contradicted; by old Baroness Puckler, for example, another who has lost great estates but does not repine. She speaks to Lushington with traditional aristocratic tolerance. Ortrud's husband is a clever man with important work: 'It is very necessary for his sake that she should be kept contented' (30). The violence of the modern world is also seen as traditional. Numbers of people have always been thrown into the river 'at times of public excitement' (3). Violent events, leading to the shooting of Da Costa and Ortrud, are more of a feature of this novel than is usual in Powell. Some passages are reminiscent of Saki. Lushington discusses with Scherbatcheff recent demonstrations at the Nikolai bridge, from which the Count's grandmother was thrown by members of the Social-Democratic party.

> 'And when the Independence was declared I suppose they threw the Bolsheviks in?'
>
> 'By that time,' Count Scherbatcheff said, 'it was winter. Holes had to be cut in the ice.'

Anti-Bolshevik animus in Powell is under proper restraint. He has none of Saki's or Evelyn Waugh's relish for thoughts of violence, although he shares their interest in how detached and amused people can be about it. This appears in the coexistence of extremely polite and formal behaviour together with ferocity. Powell implies that this is how civilisation tends to be, even if not often in England – a point on which all the non-English characters insist. Baroness Puckler explains to Lushington why so many people want to kill General Kuno. He shot great numbers of Bolsheviks during the troubles, and great numbers of other people too, because 'in those days it was hard to tell'. She concludes: 'He is the head of police too. That may cause him to be disliked by some persons' (15). These are the last words of the chapter. The pointed lack of comment is typical of the novel's method. Any connection between its events and the general state of Europe in 1932 is for readers to make themselves.

Venusberg is not a satirical novel, except in a loose sense that would cover most social comedy. Count Bobel illustrates very plainly a view pervasive in Powell's later work, that bad taste goes with moral insensitivity. He cannot be regarded as an object of satire, however. Rivalling the monsters of Gogol and Petronius, he is for the reader a source of amusement rather than dismay. Lushington has to suffer him directly, wincing at the coronet embroidered on his shirt in mauve silk, turning away from the smoke wafted from the amber cigarettes and from the bonfires left in ashtrays, declining samples of the face-cream the Count sells, noting from an old lady's demeanour as she dances with him that she is paying for their evening, politely evading all his demands, including one for girls' addresses in the industrial towns of Yorkshire. Bobel amuses us because Powell has had so much fun creating him. He acts his role of Vulgarity with the shameless high spirits of a Vice in Tudor drama; even as he is driven from the sitting-room, he is trying to show Lushington a set of comic postcards. Looking back, we can see him as an early experiment with the monomaniacal characters who, throughout the subsequent novels and especially in *Dance*, flourish by the power of the will. The valet, Pope, and his master Da Costa are further examples. In Pope will-power is hideous. It is subtler in Da Costa, who possesses a strange and to him beguiling immunity to Pope's personality, so strong for others that it can 'mess up' a whole room, although without affecting him. This gives Da Costa 'a sense of power that was rare to him' and he encourages Pope unscrupulously.

The *New Statesman*'s hostile reviewer of 1932 complained that

Powell has 'a terrible habit of making far-fetched comparisons'. The habit, to develop so richly in later books, is already a pleasure in *Venusberg*, where Mavrin, for example, looking noble in his dressing-gown, is like one of the Burghers of Calais (12). There are also early ventures with 'as if': Da Costa 'laughed again, deafeningly, as if he were going to go off his head at any moment' (10). Another pleasure which must have made attentive readers remember Powell's name is the unfailing skill with talk, notable in this book, especially in Mavrin, in those who speak English well but as a foreign language.

From a View to a Death (1933) is an entertaining redeployment of the craft developed in the first two novels. It has a new setting, English 'county' life. Vernon Passenger of Passenger Court has two daughters: Betty, in retirement after a disastrous marriage to an Italian duke, and Mary who, recently 'out', knows little of the world. His neighbour Major Fosdick has two sons, Jasper, who was in the army in the last war and now plays golf, and Torquil, home from Oxford. Mrs Brandon, a widow, has a daughter of Mary's age, Joanna. These people and their neighbours hunt, visit, quarrel and sometimes, perhaps, marry. Torquil's proposal to throw a cocktail party at the Fox and Hounds causes excitement. Mr Passenger pursues his feud with Major Fosdick, who is tenant of North Copse and shoots birds which stray there from Passenger land. Jasper is in love with Joanna who avoids him, preferring Torquil 'if a choice had to be made' (1). All so far is very familiar to readers of earlier English fiction, including the social hairs Powell likes to split. There is a frankness about sexual oddity, however, which many of the characters would think improper in a novel. Betty is attracted chiefly by homosexual men and likes the effete Torquil. Major Fosdick relaxes by sitting in his room smoking his pipe and reading a book while dressed in women's clothes. There is also a sour, uncomfortable note in many passages dwelling on the ugliness and dullness of country life.

'Why don't writers only write about the beautiful things in life?' demands Mrs Brandon (2). She and most of the other rural characters laugh nervously at the term 'high-brow', which the novel's villain intrudes on them. He and it represent a dangerous and alien culture. Powell put his middle-brow characters in their place with gentle mockery. Mrs Brandon praises her late husband:

> And he *was* the most wonderful man, Joanna. So tall and strong and sunburned. He looked like a Greek god. I remember saying that to Vernon Passenger and him saying, 'And he used to behave like one too.' Wasn't that a tribute? From someone as critical as Vernon Passenger, too. (2)

Middle-brow reading habits are observed with amusement. When Major Fosdick sits alone in Ascot picture-hat and black sequin evening dress, his book is *Through the Western Highlands with Rod and Gun* (1). Mr Passenger, who once edited, very badly, a minor seventeenth-century poet, afterwards developed 'a distaste for the life of the mind' and is now to be found reading *The Powers and Duties of Local Authorities in Connection with Rural Amenities* (1). Concepts are also limited. When Major Fosdick grumbles about Passenger's arrogance as a landowner, his wife thinks that he is 'being a bolshevik' (2). Slang limits the sporting characters. A bearded man seen by Jasper as he 'barges' about is 'the merchant with the beaver' (2). Wearing a beard is, in itself, incomprehensibly unconventional.

The beard belongs to Zouch, a high-brow portrait-painter who has been invited to Passenger Court by Mary, whom he has recently captivated. His London sophistication makes a contrast with the country folk, although this is not to his advantage. He is introduced in the first chapter, as a modern version of the Man of the Will:

> Zouch was a Superman. A fair English equivalent of the Teutonic ideal of the *Übermensch*. No one knew this yet except himself. That was because he had not been one long enough yet for people to find out. They would learn all in good time; and to their cost.

Nietzsche's philosophy of the *Übermensch* and the pursuit of power unhampered by morality is cited by Count Bobel when he tells Lushington that girls, like cigars, should be discarded when the best has been enjoyed: 'It is the sentimental who do most harm in this world of ours. You are no doubt familiar with the works of Nietzsche?' (34). Zouch is equally determined not to be sentimental. He is a weightier and so a nastier character, and, unlike Bobel, he has an antagonist, because Mr Passenger is also a superman. Joanna is the first to learn about Zouch's ruthlessness.

He seduces her and then becomes engaged to Mary. Trying to placate his father-in-law to be, he offers to ride to hounds. Passenger mounts him on Creditor, 'a playful little rogue', and at the end of the penultimate chapter Zouch, the fortune-hunter foxed, lies dead on a frosty road.

The title is from the traditional fox-hunting song 'John Peel', which is quoted in the epigraph:

> From a find to a check, from a check to a view,
> From a view to a death in the morning.

That the Nietzschean amoralist should be reduced to a 'Cockney adventurer' in the view of the Master of Foxhounds, and dealt with accordingly as though in the days of Surtees (a favourite author of Powell's), may remind us of the world of Evelyn Waugh. There are passages in this novel which have the conspicuous epigrammatic polish of Waugh: 'He was an easygoing landlord, very popular with the cottagers because he had once spoken over the wireless on an agricultural subject' (1). It is possible that each influenced the other a little. Mr Passenger sometimes seems to foreshadow Pinfold (Waugh's self-portrait) in *The Ordeal of Gilbert Pinfold* (1957): 'Mr Passenger stood on the outskirts of the group, scowling at everybody, undecided how to behave to show to the fullest advantage the disapproval he felt for his family and their acquaintances' (2). That is reminiscent of Waugh himself (also glimpsed, perhaps, in the minor character of Wauchop in *Afternoon Men*), and is a passage of pure fun. Many other scenes are painful, ugly, melancholy, and often funny at the same time in a way recalling another of Powell's near contemporaries, Graham Greene (*Stamboul Train*, 1932), without suggesting that either influenced the other. The Orphans, a band of middle-aged half-wits who play the music at Torquil's cocktail party until one of them loses his self-control, could easily have ruined a party in a Greene novel or helped to build up melancholy in a Greenean landscape, had Greene heard or thought of such a group. The butler whom Zouch rams head to head when retreating in the dawn from Joanna's room, and the chain-smoking neurotic Betty, could easily find places in Greene's world. These comparisons imply that Powell was not completely sure of finding his way with such bizarre material. The scene where Mr Passenger discovers Major Fosdick in female costume is grotesque, sad, funny and disconcerting; but it is raw and unfocused by the standards of later work.

Agents and Patients (1936) is as witty and observant as its predecessors, but the strictures of the novelist Seán O'Faoláin in his *Spectator* review are understandable, at least as first impressions:

> Mr Powell is wittily facetious in his satire on modern journalists, picture-dealers and cinema folk .... But I read *Agents and Patients* ten days ago: I know that I chuckled over it: and not another thing do I remember, except that as I read it I came on this quotation in Maurois' *Etudes Anglaises* and applied it mentally to Mr Powell. 'A humorist who does not see that his ridiculous characters live very seriously is the dupe of his own egoism'.[43]

These charges could not be brought against *From a View to a Death*, where the transformation of Zouch, from a fox sniffing about the chickens into the wretched hunted creature at the close, is most memorable, and where the Fosdick brothers are more grotesque because of the slow purposefulness behind their silly goings-on. Pringle, solemn but fatuous in his attempt at suicide, and Mavrin the innocent psychologist, are clowns who live very seriously, and they stay in the memory. *Agents and Patients* has as many grotesque figures as any of the earlier books but they are all puppet-like, with little or no inner life, which may be the reason why Seán O'Faoláin forgot them all so soon.

Agents and Patients is a more interesting novel, none the less, than was recognised in that review. Powell's enjoyment in writing about his characters and their antics, in the first three novels, allows him to be entertaining about almost anything; even trivial matters are enlivened by his way of looking at them. A girl's inept uncorking of a bottle of wine can be a memorable comic incident. There are also some passages that find new perspectives on conventionally farcical situations, as where Mavrin chats with Lushington or where Bobel guffaws at Lushington's bedroom door. *Agents and Patients* goes further, consistently asking us to look thoughtfully at farce rather than just to laugh, while discovering amusement in unexpected features of conventionally funny types of scene.

More than any of the earlier books, *Agents and Patients* looks, in summary, like the work of 'a professional humorist' – a term

Powell has disclaimed.[44] The publishers' advertisement for the Penguin edition (1984) calls it 'hilarious': 'Young Blore-Smith, just down from Oxford, views life with about as much confidence as a non-swimmer about to walk the plank'. That jaunty note, appropriate for P. G. Wodehouse, is quite alien to the tone in which the novel is told. The story seems hilarious, a contemporary treatment of the old joke: a rich young fool is shown life by clever rogues. Chipchase, a self-appointed psychoanalyst, and Maltravers, a would-be film director, persuade Blore-Smith to pay for a course of psychoanalysis, with practical lessons in life, and to finance a psychoanalytical film. The cure involves a stay in Paris, paid for by the patient, and a stay in Berlin where Maltravers has a job with a ludicrously Germanic film company. Various lively eccentrics are encountered, notably Gaston de la Tour d'Espagne, an opium-eating marquis, and Mrs Mendoza, another of Powell's monomaniacs. Gaston and his milieu alarm Blore-Smith, who flees Paris after a misadventure with a tart who steals his wallet; Mrs Mendoza carries him off from Berlin and drags him in her wake around England, paying her bills, until he is recaptured by Chipchase and Maltravers who take him to the country house of Schlumbermayer, an art-dealer planning to buy the de la Tour d'Espagne collection. Mrs Mendoza's furious husband arrives. Maltravers and Chipchase shoot the ensuing action for the psychoanalytical film. Blore-Smith escapes from all his persecutors, an agent for once as he takes the initiative to do so, but only to find refuge from the harrowing demands of real life in the quiet lodgings where we first met him.

One of Powell's techniques for flattening the high spirits of all party-going is his close attention to the pains and discomforts, embarrassments and boredom to which such pursuits are liable. He is especially good at charting the stages of Blore-Smith's drunkenness on his night out in Paris, from tipsiness to collapse, without denying the pleasures of drink but showing how thin and befuddled they can be. Blore-Smith in 'sheer lightness of heart', after dinner, fits in an extra calvados while Chipchase is out of the room. He boasts of his analyst and his partner in films. He wonders at the erotic murals at the nightclub Chez Zouzou. He speaks his few words of French to the girl Yoyo. His most acute sensation of the outing is caused by somebody's pressing the corn on his foot during the long taxi-ride from one hotel to another. When he wakes next day, robbed by Yoyo and tormented by the voice of the hotel boots,

> *Elle avait de tout petits tétons*
> *Que je tâtais à tâtons...*

the effect is free of moralistic reproach but filled with Powell's melancholy amusement at the facts of dissipation. Mixed with it, in the Paris scenes and those in Germany which follow, is an amused distaste, as where the homosexual Colonel Teape inspects Blore-Smith.

> Colonel Teape took a single eyeglass from his pocket and began to polish it with his silk handkerchief as if he wanted to make a more expert assessment of Blore-Smith's appearance than was possible even after prolonged staring with the naked eye. (2)

The fierce insistence in this sentence on the character's rudeness is made more effective by its air of light whimsy. Blore-Smith thinks Teape 'a gentleman of the old school' because the Colonel disapproves, at the nightclub, of the presence of girls. At the close of the novel Colonel Teape is trying to take control of Blore-Smith. The reader is unlikely to care what will happen because the characters are so little to be taken seriously; but the Colonel's dismal, sinister, crude presence helps to dispel hilarity while suiting Powell's austere, detached enjoyment of the rackety goings-on.

The scene that embodies the title theme is another example of how this novel avoids or deflates obvious opportunities for comedy and seeks amusement in oblique points of view. Two street entertainers, in Chapter 1, perform the roles of tormentor and victim for a group of bystanders who include the powerful agents Chipchase and Maltravers, and the hapless patient, Blore-Smith. ('He that is not free is not an Agent but a Patient', the novel's epigraph, is from one of Wesley's sermons.) One of the performers prods, with a blunt sword, his partner who lies chained at his feet. The swordsman directs melodramatic threats at the prisoner, while urging the onlookers to pay up: 'Come on, isn't there a gent among the lot of you to give a poor fellow more than one and eightpence?' (1). Evelyn Waugh would have made the most of that incongruity of tones, building up a Dickensian comic crescendo. Powell declines to do so. Instead he makes a small comedy out of the predictable ways in which chains are interpreted by the characters who watch. Chipchase and Maltravers, the novel's principal agents, think first of the political symbol. '"Rousseau was right," Chipchase said, "as regards chains."' It is only facetiously that the chained man is allowed to be a symbol for Blore-Smith's condition as a rich, bored young man. The comic point is the contrast of the tremendous physical effort of the performer, blue with cold, to free himself physically, and the facile intellectual interpretation: 'Blore-Smith walked away, ruminating on what he had seen. It had given him food for thought. He too felt himself chained. Chained by circumstance.' The killing of the metaphor by these short 'ruminating' sentences prepares for the scene soon to follow when Maltravers begins to ensnare the 'patient', Blore-Smith. They discuss the performer in chains:

'. . . How like all of us.'
'Did you think so too?'
'Psychologically speaking.'

These lines are diverting as the first snare in the entrapment of the gull, but they are even more amusing in their mockery of the symbol, inevitable and banal as symbols tend to be when reduced to conversation.

Other features of *Agents and Patients* are more interesting to those who know how they were to develop in the postwar novels than they can have been for its first reviewers. Jargon, mostly psychological here, is amusing as an incongruous element in everyday talk. 'I think I'm rather nervy', Blore-Smith confesses in Chapter 1; in Chapter 4 he confides, 'I'm rather a neurotic subject'. His innocent acceptance of Freudian terms and Chipchase's assertive use of them against him are early signs of the relish for bogusness which later produced much richer comic scenes in *At Lady Molly's* where St John Clarke practises the Marxist talk he has been taught by Quiggin. Seán O'Faoláin might have remembered some of the novel's imagery. The man in chains is said to recall 'some high-renaissance picture of Jacob wrestling with the Angel, in which the Angel is not pictorially represented, being suggested only by the contortions of Jacob' (1). The very careful and thorough working out of an incongruous comparison between raw life and fine art is only a tentative venture compared to the great flights of simile to be launched by Nick Jenkins; he would not have abandoned Jacob after a mere sentence. It belongs, none the less, with the other experiments with comic technique in *Agents and Patients*: they are stages on the way towards *A Dance to the Music of Time*.

There are two new developments in *What's Become of Waring* (1939): its plot, of a complexity Powell did not attempt again; and its first-person narrator, Nick Jenkins's closest prototype. The title is from Robert Browning's 'Waring', quoted in the epigraph:

> What's become of Waring
> Since he gave us all the slip,
> Chose land-travel or seafaring,
> Boots and chest or staff and scrip,
> Sooner than pace up and down
> Any longer London town?

Powell invented a Waring: Alec Pimley, a black sheep, exiled by his family. Pimley has chosen Toulon, where he supplements the small remittances from home by means of 'travel books' which he concocts and publishes, with moderate success, under the name of T. T. Waring. The narrator tells the story of the quest for Waring.

A summary of the main plot shows Powell's liking for coincidence and for hints that some occult influence may be at work in them. The (unnamed) narrator has a job as reader with Waring's London publisher, Judkins and Judkins. Hugh Judkins takes him to a seance at the home of a Mrs Cromwell, where the medium, in touch, it is believed, with the spirit of George Eliot, squeaks *'Tee Tee'*, a message which seems to prophesy Waring's death, announced in the newspapers next day. At the seance he meets Captain 'Tiger' Hudson, a young army officer who loves Waring's books and hero-worships the great traveller. It is from Hudson, engaged to Beryl Pimley, that the narrator first hears of Alec – whom Hudson knew at school. Judkins and Judkins appoint Hudson to write Waring's biography. Roberta Payne, a girl who likes rich men, has recently been staying at Toulon where she found out, she reports, that Waring is living there and calling himself Robinson. Eustace Bromwich, another friend from Toulon, also remembers Robinson. Hudson's preliminary research shows, disconcertingly, that Waring's adventures in Ceylon have been lifted from an obscure old book of travels. Hudson joins the narrator on holiday with Eustace in Toulon where further literary digging persuades them that all Waring's books are clever plagiarisms. Alec now turns up alive and prosperous, on a luxury yacht. He has renamed himself Alec Mason and married the former Mrs Cromwell. Eustace identifies 'Robinson', and Alec confesses to Hudson that his elderly wife's money has freed him from the need of Waring, whose death he reported to the press. He sails away with Mrs Mason, on a dangerously stormy night, to avoid further awkwardness. There is an aftermath in London. Eustace announces at the end that Alec and his wife were drowned in the storm.

There are further coincidences. The narrator used to know the Pimleys – Alec apart – and, with Hudson, comes to know them again. He learns that Alec's grandfather published, anonymously, the travels in Ceylon that Alec cannibalised for Waring's first book. In a subplot Beryl's difficult sister Winefred pursues an Indian, Mr Lal, who appears as a medium at the end of the book and 'sees' by clairvoyance aspects of the Waring story. The sceptical reader is almost but not quite free to rationalise out the occult. The medium at the earlier seance may have heard an early report of Waring's death. Nobody can know, however, that Mrs Cromwell is already secretly engaged to Alec or that Alec is T. T. Her presence is a very finely contrived coincidence. The absurdity of its being the spirit of George Eliot which issues this prophetic squib is a good enough joke to dispel most of the psychic fog, but Powell leaves the amusing, odd coincidences, as he does those of later novels, to tease us. The crowded, apparently fateful plot of the last prewar novel may help to explain, however, why Powell chose to start a long sequence when he returned to fiction after the war. He was presumably less than fully serious when he told an interviewer in 1961 that he had 'no talent for inventing plots of a dramatic kind in a comparatively short space – 80,000 words', but *What's Become of Waring* may have persuaded him that the space of a single novel was too artistically confined for his characters' dance to time's music.

The narrator has a sure but tolerant eye for absurdities, which makes him a good observer of the small publishing office – not unlike Duckworth's as described in *Messengers of Day* – a source of fun rather than a target of satire. Waring's books recount fake travellers in woolly writing, but they sell and Hugh Judkins will not hear a word against them. This is preposterous as the narrator implies, and also, as he says, reasonable because Hugh is a businessman. These two points of view, whether or not compatible, easily coexist in the quiet ironic prose. The narrator also has the inquisitive, sharp, sympathetic eye for character which was to come to life again in Nicholas Jenkins. He is good at showing the uniqueness of people who conform to social types. Minhinnick, an old, high-brow hack-writer, who appears in only one scene, conveys a whole region of the literary world of his time, one that readers of *Dance* may easily imagine that of St John Clarke. He, like General Pimley, Eustace Bromwich and others, is brought to life by his talk: 'I was saying that I wondered whether he was any relation to the Waring who wrote *Fabian Days and Fabian Ways*. I used to know him before he went under, poor fellow' (3). By the end of his few pages, Minhinnick (his name well-chosen) has broken out of the narrator's attempt to type-cast him as an 'old hack' and become an individual to remember, not as 'an eccentric' or because he belongs as he does to a particular subspecies within the genus of 'hack', but because he embodies his role with such absolute conviction and robustness that we feel nobody else could ever have been so excellent an example. The novel-sequence was later to explore the categories of shabby men-of-letters and to create equally representative and peculiar characters out of them.

Another respect in which *What's Become of Waring* looks ahead to the postwar novels is in the shaping, within the plot, of a good story. The circumstances of Hudson's appointment to write Waring's biography make an anecdote funny in itself and revealing about publishers. *Waring*'s narrator shapes this story with a care for its design worthy of his successor. After the news of the great traveller's death, Hugh and his elder brother Bernard put forward rival candidates to write the biography, neither in the least suitable except as a means to vex the opposing partner. Hugh favours a flamboyant young man, author of romantic 'historical reconstructions', Shirley Handsworth, although Shirley's manner embarrasses him. Bernard backs Minhinnick. The conflict rages for a while until deadlock is reached, and Hudson appointed as a compromise. Hugh, obliged to placate Shirley with a contract for his autobiography, is surprised that Bernard offers no objection. Minhinnick, it appears, has been offered the same recompense.

> Both authors were now at work on the stories of their respective lives. Shirley's career must have included some curious and entertaining episodes, though it was unlikely that any of these would be mentioned. Minhinnick's existence, on the other hand, had been passed in a state of dullness that rivalled that of Bernard Judkins himself. (5)

Such passages, where the phrasing gets the best of the comedy from a carefully planned climax, are among the most amusing and lifelike in Powell.

Sexual behaviour of many kinds is observed with ironic but not unkind amusement in all the early novels, without needing to state what the writing indirectly implies. The reader gathers that Shirley Handsworth's 'unpredictable expenses' arise from homosexual adventures and that Roberta Payne is (in the phrase Mr Deacon always uses in *Dance*) a *poule de luxe*, who has faked the county background she talks about almost convincingly. She deceives Waring, for a time, into thinking her rich enough to marry. Disillusioned, he prefers Mrs Cromwell to the alternative of earning a living. Eustace remarks that he did not seem the marrying sort. She has, in the meantime, sabotaged the two respectable 'shy' bachelors, Hugh Judkins, long a schoolmaster, and Tiger Hudson, engaged to a sensible dull girl. Both fall 'madly in love' with Roberta, thinking her a lovely schoolgirl. Wanting a free holiday, she goes with Hugh on his Scandinavian cruise. Neither man is well advised to play with her fire. Hudson loses his fiancée, and joins the Camel Corps when Waring also fails him. Hugh suffers a nervous breakdown, reverting to the fierce puritanism of his forebears, incompatible with successful publishing in the present day, and finally returns to schoolmastering. Eustace, who loves danger and marries often, inherits some money at the end of the story and, deservedly, marries Roberta.

Throughout the early novels there is an interest, to reach its full development only in *A Dance to the Music of Time*, which is given a special emphasis in the first and last chapters of *What's Become of Waring*. The narrator is a Stendhalian, working on his book, *Stendhal; and Some Thoughts on Violence*. This is an interest he shares with Hugh Judkins, in whom 'I suspected a sympathy with Stendhal's belief that power was the foremost of the pleasures' (1). In the novel's last paragraph the narrator broods as he tries to fall asleep, and, from the first phase of Powell's fiction, has the last word on life:

> It was power Hugh wanted too. Everybody wanted power. Bernard wanted power. Lipfield wanted power. Roberta wanted power. T. T. Waring wanted power. Did Eustace want power? It was an interesting question.

Magic and coincidence, idiosyncracy and social role, egotism and the will-to-power, and sexuality – orthodox or not – are some of Powell's themes in the 1930s which were to dominate his later novels. The power and oddness of Time are not yet fully apparent. Powell would not wish us to regard themes in his work too earnestly, however. *Waring*'s narrator has, after three years' work, not yet completed his second chapter, 'Laughter is Power'. That is more characteristic of Powell's approach to theory than the reiteration of 'power' in the novel's last paragraph. The comic balance of power between the Judkinses reflected in the two authors put to work on their unsaleable biographies is a better reminder, too, of the continuity in outlook which links *Waring* and the novels of *Dance*, where Nicholas Jenkins mocks all those who lust for power. It is a reminder also that some of Jenkins's narrative arts and features of style already existed in 1939.

3

A Dance to the Music of Time: First Person

> 'It doesn't do to read too much,' Widmerpool said. 'You get to look at life with a false perspective. By all means have some familiarity with the standard authors. I should never raise any objection to that. But it is no good clogging your mind with a lot of trash from modern novels.' . . .
>
> There was not much for me to say in reply.

This encounter, in Chapter 3 of *A Question of Upbringing* (1951), is the beginning of a debate which lasts throughout the twelve volumes of *A Dance to the Music of Time*. The sequence can be seen as a massive reply, a work written 'against Widmerpool', a defence of fiction, literature, the imaginative life, the narrator's mild, speculative, sceptical, poetic, humanist habits of mind, against everything that Widmerpool represents.

The choice of first-person narrative, which *Faces in My Time* says 'was preferable in dodging the artificiality of the invented "hero" who speaks for the author', was crucial to the whole enterprise. *What's Become of Waring* is told in a narrative voice in which Powell felt at home, while not entirely bound to create a self-portrait. Nicholas Jenkins grew from there. The opening two paragraphs of *A Question of Upbringing* reveal how much more scope the new narrator has. In contrast to the reserved 'I' of *Waring*, and the even more laconic third-person narrators, Jenkins launches his story in a full flow of impressions, memories mixed with thoughts and fancies, his long complex sentences also a contrast to the customary terseness of the earlier books. Workmen at a street-corner are like comedians, the narrator thinks, perhaps in Shakespeare; the snow falling on them puts him in mind of legionaries in the ancient world, or of centaurs, or of the figures of the Seasons in Nicolas Poussin's painting *A Dance to the Music of Time* (described but not named), where Time plays music, as for all mortals who circle stumblingly, perhaps in 'meaningless gyrations'. The classics make him think, too, of schooldays, and so the opening scenes are introduced. The central principle has already been declared: the narrator's freedom to let his mind wander; for any thought that arises to be followed wherever it leads. At the same time, this brief prelude implies a strong sense of order, confirmed as the work progresses by the series of well-shaped stories from Jenkins's last year at school, early ventures into the adult world at the homes of friends, a visit to France, and scenes from life at 'the University'. As we should expect, the first aim throughout is to entertain readers who, unlike Widmerpool, enjoy stories and character portraits, and to please readers who have a sense of form. Close attention is needed as before, and as in good traditional fiction – from Laurence Sterne, say, to Henry James – but 'difficulties' are admitted and discussed by the narrator, rather than offered, in the manner of some Modernist writing, for the reader to solve or wonder about alone. It is clear that Jenkins's account of his life will have design, but no plot of the kind Pip relates, for example, in *Great Expectations*. It is also clear that a major part of the design will belong to the narrator's commentary, a feature of older fiction largely excluded from the prewar novels and here boldly reinstated and enlarged. Anecdotes are mingled with 'scenes' of luncheons, parties, outings, as in *Afternoon Men*, but here they are surrounded and interspersed by Jenkins's brooding reflections, by his ample quotations, and by imagery done with a stately assurance. One contrast with older fiction is obvious: where Victorian narrators, even in the first person, tended to be omniscient, Jenkins is often puzzled, both about exactly what happened and about how to interpret. But he is completely in charge of his own story, digressing, interrupting himself, changing the subject, with no fussy Victorian apologies to the reader. In this respect he is closer to a typical seventeenth-century writer – Robert Burton, John Aubrey or Sir Thomas Browne – who takes for granted that he is absolute master in his own text. By the end of the first novel, Powell has persuaded us that however wayward his method seems, his narrative deserves its ruling-image of the dance, not only in the patterned comings and goings of the already large cast of characters, but also in the confident artistry of the telling.

'I was surprised, continuing to feel that I should like to know more of Sunny Farebrother' (2): surprised curiosity about others is the keynote of Jenkins as a schoolboy and undergraduate in *A Question of Upbringing*, and to some extent that of the narrator, who often comments on the *naïvete* of his younger self, but who remains inquisitive and open-minded. The last sentence of Chapter 2 tells us that more than twenty years have passed since the period the novel surveys, from late 1921 to 1924, taking Jenkins from sixteen to twenty; and there are other indications that the narrator is looking back from about 1950. Other characters are remembered with a blend of fresh interest and mature amusement.

These qualities are especially attractive in affairs of the heart. Peter Templer and Charles Stringham, with whom Jenkins is sharing a study at boarding-school in the first chapter, are slightly older than he is and far more advanced and effective in pursuit of girls. Templer first appears, back from a trip to London, boasting of success with a prostitute. Staying at Templer's home, Jenkins dances for a few moments with the widowed Lady McReith and experiences a 'revelation' of hitherto unimagined possibilities: 'my chief emotion was surprise' (2). At the same house-party he falls in love with Templer's sister Jean, cherishing her, however, only in his thoughts. Templer, he learns by accident, has spent the night with Lady McReith. At La Grenadière, the Touraine guest-house where he works on his French, there is a girl called Suzette who seems so like Jean that the two merge, confusingly, in Jenkins's mind. Determined to declare his love before leaving, he memorises a suitable speech in French, but carelessly seizes the hand of another guest, Madame Dubuisson, who has borrowed Suzette's straw hat. Too late to withdraw, he completes the speech and, perhaps – memory fails – kisses Madam Dubuisson. She receives his tribute serenely, granting permission to send her from England a picture of Buckingham Palace. Relieved and pleased, 'I began to feel quite warmly towards her', and although a little ashamed when Suzette squeezes his hand at parting, 'the passage with Madame Dubuisson seemed at any rate a slight advance in the right direction' (3). Stendhal would have approved, scientifically, of these rapid transfers of earliest passion, and of the softly ironic precision: '*slight* advance'. Stendhalians will also admire the objective manner that allows this incident its weight, although inadequate, when Stringham later boasts of his night with a divorced wife in Nairobi: 'in spite of Madame Dubuisson, this story made me feel very inexperienced' (4).

If seduction considered as a science is a theme that the older Jenkins treats playfully, power as the foremost of pleasures is announced, with more emphasis than in the early novels, as a major theme to be studied at length. His first discoveries and mistakes, in adult life, come from dealings with egoists and characters who lust for power. Monsieur Dubuisson at La Grenadière, an assertive French intellectual, is one of the egoists. Jenkins says that he had not yet grasped how such an egoist assumes that everyone else sees him as the centre of the world. Uncle Giles, who appears in this novel's first scene and its last, is a different sort of egoist, a man whose personality effortlessly causes trouble. The way in which his utter disregard for other people is revealed in his handling of his cigarette in the schoolboys' study, in Chapter 1, while applauding the school rule that forbids smoking, shows how far Powell's art has developed since the crude bad manners of the fiendish smoker Count Bobel in *Venusberg*. In Stringham's mother, a millionairess, a dominating personality is hypnotically brilliant. In others, egoism fully developed as a will for power takes a stranger form.

Two characters of this kind are found in Mrs Foxe's household: her secretary Miss Tuffy Weedon and her latest husband, Commander Buster Foxe. What these two share becomes apparent to Jenkins when Sunny Farebrother, although an impressive figure with a very good war record, behaves with grovelling deference towards Peter Templer's father, a senior business associate. Jenkins is reminded of Tuffy and Buster: for all three, 'power was won by self-abasement'. One of the novel's funniest and most interesting scenes brings Miss Weedon, Buster and Mrs Foxe together with Stringham and Jenkins as the luncheon guests of Sillery, the bachelor don who 'never takes his tea without an intrigue', and builds an empire of influence through such connections. Stringham dislikes the university and wants to go down as soon as possible. Buster opposes him and Miss Weedon as always supports him. The narrator recalls with amusement how these strong-willed characters grappled with one another while he watched with polite surprise; but he allows the young

Jenkins some intuition. He sees, for example, that gender is of little significance compared to the operations of the will, so that Sillery battling against Miss Weedon seems to be female, while she grows more masculine in asserting herself. This adaptability has little to do with sexual orientation, we gather from the older Jenkins, or with Proust's idea that a woman's nature may exist in a man's body. Sex is transcended by the urge for power, a weird phenomenon, the source of incongruities that the narrator remembers as comical rather than sinister: Sillery is like Tiresias, 'predominantly male' only in outward appearance; he is like a wizard or shaman 'equipped to resist either man or woman from a bisexual vantage' (4); when Mrs Foxe and Buster arrive, he and Tuffy 'abjure' their 'hermaphroditic' powers, needed for single combat.

In the case of Widmerpool, the young Jenkins fails at first to recognise 'a Superman' (in Zouch's sense) because relentless ambition has been disguised, at school, in the ugly, unathletic object of mild ridicule, training hard for teams he would never play for. Widmerpool is also at La Grenadière to polish up his spoken French, and Jenkins, who wondered at school 'what Widmerpool was like', is even more surprised, observing him at close quarters, by his willingness to take infinite pains in small matters. Peter Templer comments at school in Chapter 1, 'I sometimes wonder whether he is a human being at all'. Templer is thinking of the fish-like face and odd movements. There are other warnings, in Widmerpool's pompous phrasing, that he is a monster on a greater scale than the grotesques of the early books. He is to develop into one of the great humbugs of literature; his fluent, toneless pomposity is, at this stage, merely entertaining. An essential clue to him, although the quest is itself a mystery, is lost on the young Jenkins because ' Even then I did not recognise the quest for power' (3).

The narrative point of view is varied in a number of ways. One is the narrator's habit of imagining how other characters might have told the story. The first pages of Chapter 2 of *A Buyer's Market* (1952), for example, consider how Uncle Giles would have regarded the two parties that occupy more than half this novel, had he been present. The first of these begins with a dinner at Sir Gavin and Lady Walpole Wilson's house in Eaton Square from which the guests go on to a dance given by the Huntercombes. Giles, who refers to himself as 'a bit of a radical', would have condemned this smart and respectable evening's entertainment, where Jenkins met Widmerpool again in 1928 or 1929, on the grounds that people who live, as Lord and Lady Huntercombe do, in Belgrave Square, have 'more money than is good for them', and too much influence when they have 'handles to their names'. Uncle Giles's dislike of the second party, at Milly Andriadis's rented house in Hill Street, also smart – perhaps more so as Prince Theodoric is present – but less respectable, would have been 'equally, as a matter of course, overwhelming'. In this case, however, he would have condemned not only wealth, but, worse, frivolity. In the course of Milly's party, the narrator brings other imagined viewpoints to bear, including that of the painter Barnby whom the young Jenkins has not yet met, and the elderly, very bad painter and (in Stringham's phrase) 'extraordinary old puss', Mr Deacon, who is at the party and comments for himself: 'Personally I should be delighted for kings, priests, armaments manufacturers, *poules de luxe*, and *hoc genus omne* to be swept into the dust-bin – and I might add all the nonsense we find about us tonight' (2). Mr Deacon has just finished telling, with keen enjoyment, a particularly scandalous story about his hostess's past career as a *poule de luxe*. A chance invitation has brought him in, for an hour of champagne and fashionable company, from the streets where he was selling *War Never Pays!* – copies left under a chair in the hall will cause trouble later on. Now he reverts to the style of these pamphlets; or, rather, to Powell's parody of the 'dustbin' vein of radical rhetoric, the Latin tag rebuking the priests and the 'luxury chicks' together. Mr Deacon is far more than a satirical butt, a character known to Jenkins since childhood and remembered with affection as well as amusement; but here he confirms the impression misanthropic Uncle Giles has been brought in to create: that all radical opinion arises from bad-temper and hypocrisy – the ruling point of view throughout the novel.

Young Jenkins works in a publisher's office, and later as a script-writer, so that Powell wrote from experience, as usual. He, too, soon becomes a novelist, and this role affects his view of the many characters who are either writers, mingling with artists and musicians, or members of the business world, which gives the second and third volumes of *Dance* their titles. Business or the arts seems the choice for most of Jenkins's school and university acquaintances, some, like the Sillery protégé Truscott, equally promising in both. Although publishing might be thought to connect the two realms, City characters do not take the book trade very seriously.

Jenkins meets Mark Members and J. G. Quiggin at Sillery's tea-parties in *A Question of Upbringing* and has dealings with both throughout the sequences. His account of the literary world in the first five volumes concentrates on the story of Members, Quiggin and St John Clarke. The presentation of Clarke reflects Jenkins's (and Powell's) sense of the 1914–18 war as the end of an era. In the novel's subjective view of history, he is antediluvian, a survivor from an utterly lost world of country-house parties given by great literary hostesses during golden summers, of big sales and solid prestige derived from – Jenkins now thinks – false romantic stories in windy prose. The fact that Jenkins, like most of the characters, enjoyed reading Clarke in childhood makes him seem no less anachronistic in the contemporary world. Members and Quiggin, drawn by his wealth, try to modernise him. Members, socially polished, making a name with his verse, an aesthetic phase already behind him, becomes Clarke's secretary in the last chapter of *A Buyer's Market*, and converts him to Modernism in *The Acceptance World* (1955). Quiggin, who is or plays the role of a raw Northern scholarship boy, outwits his rival, converting Clarke to Marxism and seizing the secretaryship, briefly regained at one point by Members, although supplanted by a committed German dramatist ('No mere entertainment, please'), Werner Guggenbühl, who converts his master to Trotskyism. St John Clarke appears at a luncheon in *Casanova's Chinese Restaurant* (1960), where his orotundity and absent-minded lapses into the style of *Queen Mary's Gift Book* make an apt setting for Powell's satire against parlour socialism. The narrator relishes the farcical aspect of these proceedings, contrasting his earlier self – surprised, interested, detached – with the resolute worldly young men for whom literature happened to serve as a convenient means to advancement and power. Jenkins is usually ready to consider the opposite side of his points of view. Having depicted Clarke and his satellites as persons only superficially resembling himself, in being writers, while separated from him in living wholly by the will, he reconsiders when he meets St John Clarke at the luncheon. Albeit a buffoon and a 'bad' writer (the term so qualified because nobody can prove it), Clarke is, perhaps, as a fellow novelist, a kindred spirit.

Coming from an army family, Jenkins enters a new milieu when he visits the home of Peter Templer in *A Question of Upbringing*, its strangeness heard in the language: Mr Templer is in cement and still doing well despite 'an appalling bloomer over steel' (his son's phrase). Nick as a child was fascinated by hearing about 'a big iron man'; he retains a lively interest in the poetic diction of finance. 'The Acceptance World', metaphorically easy to explain, has a precise City sense he keeps trying to track down. Later he can be intrigued by hearing of 'cheap money', or learning that an acquaintance is 'connected with the by-products of coal'. Business-people he meets at the Templers, including Sunny Farebrother, Bob Duport and Jimmy Stripling, take such terms for granted and would think Jenkins's literary savouring of them childish nonsense. For them the making of money, always a mystery to the narrator, is the central purpose of a man's life, and despite the good things it buys – including the distractions of golf and girls – life's foremost pleasure. Men are judged by their business abilities: Jenkins is surprised to learn that Peter, always reckoned hopeless at school, is highly regarded by the City men. Here, among people of his own class and upbringing, is an alien culture and one he respects, with misgivings. Although he can hold his own in the conversational 'rough and tumble' at the Templers', it is less congenial than the ambience at Stringham's Belgravia home – 'pompous' in Templer's terminology – where Mrs Foxe's old money is being rapidly spent; conversation there is more exacting and more fun. Tuffy has managed to get tickets for the Russian ballet. Nobody mentions golf.

The narrator is not inclined to schematise. Readers who think that *Dance* shows the disintegration of traditional England can find support in the careers, charted in the first half of the sequence, of Templer, Stringham, and Widmerpool. Templer becomes a successful stockbroker, damaged in 1929 but able to recover. Stringham joins the personal staff of the great industrialist, Sir Magnus Donners. We see him at work with his fellow secretary, Truscott, in *A Buyer's Market*, valued both for his 'charm' and his family background. In the same novel Widmerpool, devoid of either sort of claim but able and hardworking, joins Donners–Brebner; but Stringham leaves, declining into alcoholism in *The Acceptance World*. Before leaving to become a billbroker, Widmerpool ruthlessly ousts Truscott and grows formidable; the narrator is astonished to find Templer estimating him far above Stringham. It is tempting to see a significant pattern. The wit and dandy declines and the boorish outsider rises in his place. Stringham, who could have tried whatever career he wanted, chose commerce, recognising, perhaps, the crucial field of combat, because Donners presides, in Stourwater Castle, over the 1930s England pictured in these books. The John-Bull-like Templer, Stringham's friend at school, recognises the 'new man' in Widmerpool. Is this a late stage in the long struggle between noble and bourgeois? If any such design is implicit the narrator does not state or assert it. Stringham is cursed by melancholy, a disease of good minds which also touches Templer. Individuals interest Jenkins far more than movements. His distrust of categories appears in *The Acceptance World* when, weary of literati, he goes as a guest to Peter Templer's house in the stockbroker belt, looking for 'ordinary life'. After a day with Templer, his wife Mona, Jimmy Stripling, the clairvoyant Mrs Erdleigh and Quiggin, he decides, 'not for the first time, how mistaken it is to suppose there exists some "ordinary" world into which it is possible to wander at will. All human beings, driven as they are at different speeds by the same Furies, are at close range equally extraordinary' (3). The Kindly Ones hunt Stringham down more quickly, but they pursue Widmerpool and Templer, Quiggin and Members, businessmen, writers and everyone else.

Some readers may feel that Widmerpool is even more extraordinary than the other characters, and that, although he is driven by the Furies in his own nature, the novelist sometimes seems to drive him harder than he deserves. There was a danger for Powell in the use of a first-person narrator who is also the hero, opposed to an anti-hero such as Widmerpool; it is in *At Lady Molly's* (1957) that we first become aware of this threat to the integrity of the fiction. Lady Molly Jeavons gives a party early in the novel for the engagement of her friend Mildred Haycock to Widmerpool, and another, near the end, for Jenkins's engagement to her niece, Lady Isobel Tolland. Widmerpool has always been as bizarre in love as in everything else except business and administration. The first volume implies that he has a vein of masochism. Hit in the eye by a banana from the hand of the Captain of Cricket, he reacts with a look of slavish satisfaction. At the Huntercombe's ball in *A Buyer's Market*, Barbara Goring, with whom he, as well as Jenkins, is in love, pours a large castor of sugar over his head, and the same look appears – although Barbara's action kills his passion, and Jenkins's. He falls instead for Gypsy Jones, a scruffy radical girl, paying for her abortion. Mrs Haycock is even more unsuitable; ten years older, twice married, with two sons frequently expelled from school, she has 'slept with every old-timer between Cannes and St Tropez' (*At Lady Molly's*, 5). Jenkins is far more successful. He has had a long and passionate, although painful affair with Jean Duport (née Templer), in *The Acceptance World*. Meeting Isobel Tolland, eighth of the ten children of the last Lord Warminster, at the Thrubworth home of her brother Erridge, the present Earl, he knows instantly that he will marry her. A reader who has persisted thus far into the sequence likes Jenkins and must be pleased by his marriage to a well-read, intelligent woman who shares his anarchic sense of humour and tolerates, at least, his otherwise conservative cast of mind ('stuck up' is the phrase of Gypsy Jones, with whom he 'enacted the long-established rite', once, in *A Buyer's Market*, 4). Nothing other than the obtrusive sense of the author, in this case persecuting his character, could interfere with the reader's enjoyment of Widmerpool. Having begun as a buffoon, he is now more sinister as a man with some power and status, although not yet the ogre of the later books, while remaining as clownish as before. He is funny as the target of the narrator's acid way with words. Inviting Jenkins to lunch at his club in Chapter 2 of *At Lady Molly's*, he opens with the words that Kingsley Amis once said are the most depressing in the language: 'We might go straight in to lunch.' The host then orders for himself cold tongue and a glass of water. Jenkins's comment is laconic. 'I ordered all I decently could in the face of this frugality'. (The novels frequently assert that power-men dislike food and drink.) Congratulations are offered on the engagement to Mildred Haycock. 'Widmerpool bowed his head in acknowledgement. The movement could almost have been called gracious ... "I do not mind informing you that my lady mother thinks well of my choice," he said' (2). The engagement is also good fun both as a topic of conversation and as a theme for the narrator to ponder. The disparity of age is made to seem more striking because Mrs Haycock is sister-in-law to General Conyers, an old family friend of the Jenkinses, now, in 1934, almost eighty. Conyers, anxious to find out what sort of fellow is marrying Mildred, never an easy woman to 'handle', demands to be told.

Jenkins tries to explain their shared background: "Nonsense," said the General. "You can't have been at school with him". Mrs Conyers supports her husband: 'This claim to have been at school with Widmerpool was something not to be credited' (2). In such a context, Jenkins's perennial difficulty in finding formulas to express what Widmerpool is '*like*' is pushed to the limits. He cannot proceed further than his earlier judgment, when asked 'Is he nice?', that whatever other positive terms might conceivably be allowed, Widmerpool is not 'nice'. Mildred's proper handling involves strenuous pursuit of rackety entertainments, including night-clubs. Taking the solemn clown so far out of his element is the right comic course, but Powell makes one of his few misjudgments when he gives Widmerpool jaundice. Even if we accept that Widmerpool out on the town in bright yellow corresponds to Malvolio – who belongs somewhere in his literary ancestry – in yellow stockings, a robust joke about which we should not be squeamish, attention has been drawn to the author's power over his character. When the 'trial night', anxiously awaited by Widmerpool, who confers with Jenkins on the subject, turns out a fiasco, the engagement broken off, the illusion which any novel depends on is disturbed. The effect is more noticeable because Jenkins is at his most vulnerable, at this point in the story, to the reader's curiosity. We are inquisitive about his marriage, over which every sort of veil is drawn, even denying us the right novels have granted ever since the genre's bourgeois beginnings, to know about the money. There is no appeal to the 'lifelike' here: in life a Widmerpool might well be no match for Mildred Haycock; he might develop psychosomatic jaundice. A novelist must be more fair to his characters than life would be. We are entitled to jeer at Widmerpool and so is the narrator, but the author is not. It is especially unfair of him to do so while sheltering his hero.

Widmerpool's failure with Mildred is the opportunity for an especially good scene involving General Conyers, who is among the characters Jenkins most admires:

> In fact, his personality filled the room, although without active aggression. At the same time he was a man who gave the impression, rightly or wrongly, that he would stop at nothing. If he decided to kill you, he would kill you; if he thought it sufficient to knock you down, he would knock you down: if

a mere reprimand was all required, he would confine himself to a reprimand. In addition to this, he patiently maintained a good-humoured, well-mannered awareness of the inherent failings of human nature: the ultimate failure of all human effort. (2)

This is one of the passages which might serve as a credo for Jenkins; the will here is highly developed but under control; the decisiveness of a man of action, which Jenkins lacks, while people he dislikes possess it, is combined with the classical 'awareness', described in the last twenty words, shared by Jenkins and lacking in Quiggin, Sillery, Uncle Giles, Widmerpool and many others who live by will alone. 'Well-mannered' is an essential feature of Conyers as a model character. None of these latter people is ever courteous. 'Ultimate' is essential too, emphasised by the resolution in Conyers, which, it seems ('rightly or wrongly'), will stop at nothing. Despite his age and, since his retirement from the army, long years of duties at court, the General's interests are abreast of the times. He has been reading Virginia Woolf's *Orlando* (1928), puzzled but interested. In the scene in the last pages of *At Lady Molly's* he reveals a good working knowledge of the theories of Freud, rising to 'heights of scientific detachment', in analysing the case of Widmerpool, which Jenkins feels are far above his reach. The General diagnoses him, in an afterthought: 'an introverted intuitive type'. 'Exaggerated narcissism' is, perhaps, Widmerpool's trouble, although other neuroses are no doubt at work below the surface. Unlike many of the novels' younger intellectuals, Conyers is modest about his own competence to discuss what he has learned at second hand; and, while keen on his new subject, he is intelligently sceptical about all human efforts, including psychoanalysis. That moderation is one of many reasons why the young Jenkins and the narrator admire Conyers. The scene is especially impressive in being consistently funny without allowing the General to become for a moment a figure of fun.

'For my own part, I always enjoy hearing details of other people's lives, whether imaginary or not': this would make another part of Jenkins's credo. From the last chapter of *At Lady Molly's*, the words are a comment on an agreeable contemporary, Chips Lovell, a fellow script-writer who is related to many branches of the aristocracy, and is an enthusiastic gossip. Chips's chatter at the Studio could have given offence, Jenkins reflects, since many people feel such talk 'to derogate their own importance, few being interested in how others live' (5). This is one of the more challenging views offered in *Dance*, inquisitive and gossiping instincts being, it is usually thought, commonplace. As though to indicate the true interest he and Lovell share, the same paragraph refers to the 'strange, lifeless, formalised convention to illustrate human experience' usually found in people of the film world. We might also remember Mrs Brandon and Mrs Dodds, in *From a View to a Death*, who have made a treaty to gossip in equal 'innings', suffering no derogation of importance because neither listens to a word the other says. A part of the true interest in others' lives is memory for trivial details, a passion for Lovell and Jenkins; its loss, in Stringham and Templer in the years after leaving school, is the saddest aspect, in the earliest books, of Jenkins's estrangement from them. He finds later friends who are, like him, connoisseurs of gossip: Ralph Barnby the painter, accomplished womaniser and fund of lore about women – also an expert on Mr Deacon; and the composer and conductor, Hugh Moreland.

Moreland first appears in *Casanova's Chinese Restaurant* although he has been a friend since Mr Deacon introduced him at the period covered in *A Buyer's Market* (1928/9). Moreland is in many respects at the furthest extreme from the characters who live by the will and pursue power. They tend to be humourless and limited in interests; he is among the most witty and erudite people in *Dance*. By Widmerpool's criteria, he is hopeless: self-indulgent, irresolute, ambitious for his music but only waywardly for himself, diffident, a prey to melancholy, sorely in need of the managerial skills of his wife Matilda, and ill-equipped for everyday life when she leaves him. He is akin to the narrator in liking the arts and liking people for their own sake, as well as for the fun that can be had from thinking and talking about them. They are also united in certain hostilities, especially in mockery of one of *Dance*'s greatest philistines and bore, Sir Magnus Donners (for whom Matilda, formerly Donners's mistress, deserts him). Moreland has toughness, moreover, of a sort not known to Widmerpool, to be seen in the last chapter of *Casanova's Chinese Restaurant* where he proves his loyalty to his friend and fellow musician Maclintick whose desperation, soon to be followed by suicide, makes one of the grimmest scenes in the sequence. Although

Moreland lacks the force and practicality of Conyers, the narrator's regard for his closest friend could be expressed in his words of praise for the General, granted that originality as a composer corresponds to 'stopping at nothing'.

Several generally well-disposed reviewers of this fifth volume expressed doubts about Jenkins's ability to sustain the sequence further, given his role as a very detached onlooker. Evelyn Waugh, in the *Spectator*, found much to praise, especially Mrs Foxe's party for Moreland's symphony, where Stringham reappears and tames Maclintick's shrewish wife – one of the best scenes in all Powell. Waugh makes a useful contrast between the world of *Dance* and the world of Graham Greene, whose characters 'never know anybody' and live 'under the solitary eye of God'.[45] Powell's people are acquainted with almost everybody, although nobody knows anyone else well enough. Jenkins knows everyone, but nobody as well as he would like, and in other respects he is not in the least a godlike narrator. He enjoys observing how 'everyone's path crosses and recrosses everyone else's' but he does not lay down a philosophy. He and most of his friends are now married or, like the homosexual actor Norman Chandler with whom Mrs Foxe falls in love, breaking up marriages. Waugh declares that Jenkins's authority as narrator is weakened by his lack of any 'solid' belief. (He plainly regretted Powell's lack of faith.) While keeping his own marriage out of the story, Jenkins tells us that other people's marriages are impossible to analyse. The fifth volume of *Dance*, Waugh fears, has lost direction; the sequence has entered a phase of 'apparent stagnation'.

V. S. Pritchett wrote the *New Statesman*'s review in the same week (25 June 1960). Pritchett praised the quality of melancholy 'grimly engrained' in the comedy, arguing that 'when one speaks of his melancholy one is not describing a passive condition; one is speaking of a driving force'. The danger was, however, that the 'deep spate' of the early books might drift in 'the shallows': 'what began as a panorama begins to sound like a gossip column'.

> One has the irritating impression that Jenkins, the narrator, has no other profession but to run about collecting the news; his stability has become fitful. The characters exchange too much hearsay. This is the danger with the *roman fleuve* when it lacks a strongly sustaining idea beyond the convenience of

its own existence.[46]

These opinions, from technicians of fiction of the highest calibre, may reflect misgivings in Powell's mind. The next volume, *The Kindly Ones* (1962), begins with a refreshing change. In the seventy-five pages of its first chapter, Jenkins goes back in memory to 1914 when he was a child of eight, living at the haunted bungalow Stonehurst with his parents – and with Albert the cook, Bracey the soldier–servant and Billson the parlourmaid, while out in 'the wild country' beyond the garden the frightening figure of the magician, Dr Trelawney, roams. This could be read as a self-contained 'section'; it must also be seen as the introduction to a new stage of the sequence, in which a profession is thrust on Jenkins by war. Comedy is finely engrained with melancholy in the figure of the naked Billson giving her 'notice' in the Stonehurst drawing-room on the day of General Conyers's visit: Nicholas's mother 'thought it was the end of the world'. The announcement shortly afterwards of the killing of the Archduke Franz-Ferdinand at Sarajevo (28 June 1914), closing an epoch, the narrator recalls, with its presage of war, was made by Uncle Giles, who 'did not look in the least like the harbinger of the Furies', although Dr Trelawney is in attendance. The child Nicholas has learned about 'Eumenides', whom the Greeks called the Kindly Ones to appease their wrath, from his governess; they are confused in his mind with suffragettes, whom Albert, fearing they may attack Stonehurst, calls 'Virgin Marys'.

> I recalled Miss Orchard's account of the Furies. They inflicted the vengeance of the gods, by bringing in their train war, pestilence, dissension on earth; torturing, too, by the stings of conscience. This last characteristic alone, I could plainly see, made them sufficiently unwelcome guests.

'I could plainly see' nicely puts adult worries in their place. The old Stonehurst way of life was broken up, however, ending childhood by the coming of the Great War. In the later sections of the novel, in 1939, Jenkins awaits the Furies' return: intruding into an evening of charades at Stourwater, in Chapter 2, an ungainly and menacing figure in uniform, Widmerpool is a more suitable harbinger than Uncle Giles had been. Sorting out his uncle's effects before his funeral, in Chapter 3, Jenkins finds the

Victorian commission appointing 'our Trusty and well-beloved *Giles Delahay Jenkins, Gentleman*', to be an officer of the Queen, 'According to the Rules and Disciplines of War'. There follows an extended and very funny analysis of how far short Uncle Giles had fallen of the Queen's expectations, ending abruptly with Jenkins's disquieting thought that 'No doubt irony, facile or otherwise, can often go too far.' He will himself soon be subject to 'the Rules and Disciplines of War'. The uncertainty, tinged with fears about how he will fare, although it cannot subdue for more than half a page the play of his irony, gives a new narrative interest to this volume, and to the next three which deal with the war years. It is not the theme which Evelyn Waugh foresaw; he praises *The Kindly Ones*, in his *Spectator* review, for introducing a grand argument: 'the Eumenides accomplish their task of vengeance, begun in 1914, completed in 1939, by the destruction of English civilisation'. That forecast, satisfying to Waugh, is not justified by the second half of the sequence. Powell's view of English civilisation, classic rather than romantic, is of something more complicated, impure and adaptable than Waugh likes to imagine, and constantly subject to the Furies' onslaughts. But Jenkins at war, a private man forced into the national war effort, an observer who is now obliged to accept responsibility and risk, becomes a more substantial figure than the witty gossip of *Casanova's Chinese Restaurant*. Even for readers who were completely happy so far with the wit and gossip, war offers livelier prospects for both; and as Jenkins the protagonist comes closer in maturity of outlook to the narrator, he has more of our sympathy, while remaining a cool and guarded reader's companion, now that we share the 'personal mythology' of his childhood.

According to a saying of Moreland's which the narrator quotes towards the end of *The Valley of Bones* (1964), 'it is just the way you look at things' (4). Second-Lieutenant Jenkins, serving with a Welsh regiment in the first year of the war, consoles himself amidst duties which are at best fairly uncongenial by looking at things from as many points of view as possible. The narrator constantly remembers him remembering old acquaintances, conversations, fragments of reading, which jostle in the text with the new impressions. Memories tend to be literary, intellectual, poetic, while actualities are trivial or sordid. In the novel's opening pages Jenkins's first day in Captain Gwatkin's company puts him in mind of a host of pleasant irrelevances, including his own Welsh ancestry, Celtic history and legend, El Greco, Bonaparte, the Seven Churches of Asia, Belshazzar's feast, Baudelaire, Genghis Khan, Roncesvalles, Daumier and Stendhal, while the military preoccupations of his new commander include incorrect officers' insignia, improperly folded blankets, pay-parade, ring-worm, the nominal roll and urine buckets. Jenkins recalls, from Chapter 3 of *The Kindly Ones*, the prophecy of war he heard, in farcical circumstances, from Dr Trelawney, the professional soothsayer first glimpsed and overheard in Stonehurst days, and encountered again at the boarding-house where Uncle Giles died: 'The sword of Mithras, who each year immolates the sacred bull, will ere long now flash from the scabbard'. Jenkins is amused by the sage's windy poeticism, but the same long-distance view of war that myth can afford attracts him in the passage of genuine poetry from Ezekiel 37 (from which the novel's title is drawn), read at church parade and quoted at length in the last pages of the first chapter: 'And he said unto me, Son of Man, can these bones live? . . . and the breath came unto them and they lived, and stood up upon their feet, an exceeding great army'. He wants to feel at home in the army; the effort to adjust is more of a challenge than he has ever met before. The idioms of the temporary officers, mostly bank employees, and of the other ranks, mostly miners, are unfamiliar; and so is conversation among men to whom literature – except in hymns and the Authorised Version – is almost unknown, London a remote and alien city. Gradually, listening to the commonplace conversations of the Mess, he distinguishes among his comrades different ways of looking at the army, and at life.

Rowland Gwatkin and Idwal Kedward are contrasted as representing romantic and realistic approaches. Banking careers in the Welsh Valleys have made both of them competitive and conscientious; but while Kedward, at twenty-two, a good age for a lieutenant, has a clear grasp of what running a platoon or company requires, Gwatkin, a territorial captain about Jenkins's age, 'fancies himself as a great soldier' (1). His overweening ambition, aggravated when the company moves to the Castlemallock School of Chemical Warfare in Northern Ireland by his 'sacred' love for the Irish barmaid Maureen, causes his downfall. Despite much ironic amusement, Jenkins likes his spirited conception of the soldier's role, which survives even the devastating boredom and vexation of Castlemallock – vividly conveyed in

Chapter 4. He is equally impressed, however, by Kedward's straightforward frankness on taking over Gwatkin's job. Jenkins is to be transferred away from the regiment; Kedward admits he is glad to be rid of an ageing, inexperienced subaltern without much soldierly talent. The narrator observes that he values people who deal in realities, 'provided it is always borne in mind that so-called realities present, as a rule, only a small part of the picture' (4).

Two officers who share his broader outlook, David Pennistone and Dicky Umfraville, both met while on leave in Chapter 3, offer Jenkins two theories of military life. Pennistone, a military philosopher to be encountered again in the ninth volume, tells Jenkins, who knows Alfred de Vigny only as a nineteenth-century poet, about Vigny as a veteran of the French army who believed that a soldier is 'a monk of war', dedicated to a way of life in which 'there is as little room for uncontrolled fervour as for sullen indifference'. Jenkins later tries to explain Vigny to Gwatkin and to persuade him that the 'bloody boring side' of soldiering counts most, glamour arising only as an occasional 'bit of luck'; but Vigny means nothing to Gwatkin – one of the majority of people, the narrator tells us, for whom literature cannot illumine life. Dicky Umfraville's thought is from Marshal Lyautey, who 'pacified North Africa and all that', and held that the first essential of an officer is 'gaiety'. Umfraville, a regular until he had to resign his commission, had hoped to build a career on that principle, 'not as regards neglecting the ladies, but in other respects' (the Marshal having also been 'gay' in the present, restricted sense of the word). Very few modern British officers live up to that criterion, he and Jenkins agree; although one who does, the narrator reflects, is General Liddament, observant, energetic and a striking contrast to the many bumbling senior officers encountered. Liddament shows the proper *joie de vivre*, although he is eccentric on occasion, as in the scene in Chapter 2 where he insists that all soldiers should have porridge for breakfast. Another who passes this test is Odo Stevens, an energetic young subaltern gifted in various directions, resembling Umfraville, Jenkins thinks, in being a narcissist, enthralled by his own personality, but not an egoist because equally interested in and observant of other people. Such gaiety can be dangerous: Jenkins introduces Stevens to his sister-in-law, once loved by Moreland, now Lady Priscilla Lovell, a girl above his normal social level;

she is captivated at once. When he knows Stevens better, in *The Soldier's Art* (1966), Jenkins decides that his is a true gaiety because it coexists with a true, thoughtful melancholy. One explanation of the quality Stevens and Umfraville share is that they aim to enjoy soldiering – like everything in life; this includes doing it well, promotion – or death – being secondary issues. Most of the abler officers, including Gwatkin and Kedworth, struggle for power. Few people, Jenkins reflects, 'do anything for its own sake' (4).

Widmerpool reappears at the end of *The Valley of Bones*, at the time of Italy's entry into the war in June 1940, as DAAG (Deputy Assistant Adjutant-General). It is typical of Jenkins's delight in past associations that he is glad to see this old acquaintance, and typical of their relationship that he is sorry, within a few pages, to be 'in Widmerpool's power'. Power-struggles among strong-willed, ambitious officers occupy much of the first and third chapters of *The Soldier's Art*, with Widmerpool, at the centre, intriguing against Sunny Farebrother, whose famous charm is a fearsome weapon, and the fiery-tempered Colonel Hogbourne-Johnson. They almost overwhelm Widmerpool, who escapes them at the end, promoted into the ultimate power-centre of the Cabinet Offices. These men cannot be thought of, in Jenkins's terms, as 'monks of war', since they are dedicated only to their own advancement; and they are devoid of what Marshal Lyautey meant by 'gaiety'. Jenkins is more interested in two of Widmerpool's powerless victims, Lieutenant Bithel and Private Stringham. It is only grotesquely, and in small measure, that they can be said to show the spirit of dedication or that of martial gaiety, yet they come closer to these ideals than abler men of higher rank.

Bithel, who first appears in *The Valley of Bones*, is an assembly of all the unofficerlike qualities Powell could reasonably unite in one character: an habitual drunkard, a fraud who pretends to have played rugby for Wales and to have a brother with a Victoria Cross, unreliable in dealings with 'good-looking boys' among the other ranks, careless with cheques; he is also physically unfit, easily frightened, accident-prone and in every sense inelegant. The narrator describes him with the stylistic equivalent of raised eyebrows; Lieutenant Jenkins accepts him, with his usual politeness, as a comrade at arms, and as time goes by regards him with a cool degree of the sympathy he always extends to those who have shared a part of his life. Stringham turns up again, in Chapter 1 of *The Soldier's Art*, as the new waiter in F Mess. Jenkins, now Widmerpool's assistant, dines here with some of the most uncouth junior officers, who jeer at Stringham's 'la-di-da' manner of speaking; it seems that an old friend is being humiliated beyond sufferance. Successfully cured of 'drink' by Tuffy Weedon (now married to General Conyers), Stringham has 'severed his moorings pretty completely with anything that could be called everyday life, army or otherwise' (3), but is, on the surface, more cheerful than at any time since the school scenes of *A Question of Upbringing*. Widmerpool transfers him from the Mess to the mobile laundry, now commanded by Bithel, and he says he prefers this to Jenkins's job, working for Widmerpool. Liking Bithel for being so little different drunk or sober, not 'nasty' but benevolent in drink, Stringham summons Jenkins to help him to return his incapably drunk officer safely to his quarters in Chapter 3, but Widmerpool discovers them and Bithel is 'shot out' of the army next day. 'Poor Bith', Stringham's feeling, is shared by Jenkins, who remembers the gallant-seeming although drunken dance Bithel performed, putting out of countenance those who tried to rag him on his first night, and who knows how proud Bithel was, fulfilling boyhood dreams inspired by comic-paper heroics, to command the men of the laundry. Widmerpool notes, as an odd feature of this case, that Bithel was in floods of tears when he learned his fate. Fascination with details of human behaviour, here the new information about Bithel, is so natural to Jenkins that the complete absence of any corresponding curiosity in Widmerpool alarms him. He thinks lack of pity 'reasonable' but his lack of interest in Bithel makes Widmerpool seem alien – something worse than a buffoon, a man whom power may the more easily corrupt because of his 'absolute lack of interest in human beings as such' (3). The DAAG has no interest in Stringham either, except concern lest he prove an 'embarrassment' or a threat to discipline. His decision to post Stringham to the laundry, soon to be dispatched to the Far East, seems monstrous to Jenkins – not a reaction, perhaps, which the reader is meant fully to share, since Stringham is delighted by the chance to see 'the gorgeous East'. These two men at arms are, nevertheless, sharply contrasted. Everybody finds his level in the army, Widmerpool explains; he is a Major, Jenkins a Second Lieutenant and Stringham a Private. The Private's 'poor Bithel' contrasts with the Major's dismissal of Bithel as 'the brute' (3); and Widmerpool's solemn satisfaction about his important new job contrasts with Stringham's cheerful departure for the East, the last we hear from him since he is to die in a Japanese camp in the next volume. '*Quis separabit*? – that's the Irish Guards isn't it? The Mobile Laundry share the motto.' Here, in the strongest of contrasts with Widmerpool, is a touch of the spirit Marshal Lyautey recommended.

Jenkins would have less time for military philosophising, readers may think, especially those who like fiction about war, if he practised the soldier's art in action. He never reaches a front; but in the second chapter of the second war-volume, he suffers the effects of the blitz on London. Chips Lovell and his wife Priscilla are killed in circumstances that raise questions about the author's attitude to death in its fateful – or coincidental – aspect. The evening begins at the Café Royal. Jenkins has a drink with Chips Lovell, who leaves him to go to the Café de Madrid, hoping for a reconciliation with Priscilla, who has left him for Odo Stevens. Moreland arrives for dinner, closely followed by Mrs Maclintick, with whom he is now living. Stevens and Priscilla join them by chance; Priscilla soon leaves without explanation. Back at Moreland's flat, they learn that the Madrid has been hit by a bomb, Chips being among those killed. Jenkins goes to the Jeavons's to break the news to Priscilla and finds that she and Lady Molly have been killed, by another tip-and-run bomber. We are accustomed, now, to coincidences in Jenkins's life, unsurprised that Widmerpool should be the staff-officer he works for, or that Stevens and Priscilla should happen to be at the Café Royal that night. Coincidence, in the sense that Priscilla went to meet her husband, although not at the Madrid, is a phenomenon on which we might have hoped for a comment from the narrator, who only points to another coincidence, that Chips first took him to Lady Molly's hoping to find Priscilla. This ominous background to the characters' dance increases in the volumes still to come, as death claims more of them.

The Military Philosophers (1968) emphasises a feature of the sequence that has been noticeable throughout: the narrator is interested in events for the sake of how they can be, or might be, reported. It is natural, although fiction need not follow nature in this respect, that Jenkins should hear about far more occurrences than he witnesses. That has been so from the first anecdotes Stringham relates about Widmerpool at school until the old cabaret-singer Max Pilgrim tells of the Madrid's destruction. There is an art in the selection of raconteurs in the worlds of gossip which surround the narrator; the young Stringham relishes Widmerpool as a fund of stories with a quality of appreciation that he teaches Jenkins. Max Pilgrim's camp tones, in *The Soldier's Art*, are, perhaps surprisingly, appropriate for the story of how suddenly people snatching an evening's pleasure from the gruelling effort of the war can be obliterated. Pilgrim has always been a remote, exotic figure, singing of 'Di, Di, in her collar and tie' in a voice like an octogenarian dowager's; in this scene he is an ordinary ageing theatre queen, greeting Jenkins with a 'my dear' for once muted, shocked to think of the young Germans – ungratefully he says, remembering prewar Berlin – trying to kill him. In the next volume Jenkins is no less artistic in retelling the tales he is told. But whereas Pilgrim, and elsewhere Stevens, who has been in action (winning a Military Cross) and tells Jenkins what it feels like, gives us a vivid second-hand sense of the war, *The Military Philosophers* puts the war at an even further remove. We now hear the narrator's reports of what people tell him they have heard from those waging war in the field. This can be very effective; and it is perhaps appropriate that the hero should seem out of things because he now holds an appointment at the War Office.

Jenkins still reminds himself of Lyautey's precept; when his duties as a Liaison Officer bring him in touch with the Free French, he notices that they 'do not neglect' this principle – indulging it sometimes with abandon. He finds as much scope as ever for inner frivolity, transforming in imagination the drab settings and personnel of the War Office into Wagnerian opera, in the opening pages. His new job is more demanding and interesting than the regimental chores of the last two books, requiring Vigny's dedication at a higher level than mere resistance to boredom. *The Military Philosophers* covers events from 1942 to 1945. Helping to deal with Polish affairs, Jenkins is concerned with the release into Persia of the Polish troops, held since 1939 by the Russians, who were to form the 2nd Polish Army Corps. His department is also anxious about the Polish officers, estimated between nine and fifteen thousand, whose disappearance is unexplained. Promoted, early in 1943, to be in charge of dealings with the Belgians and Czechs, Jenkins exchanges letters with the Belgians' man on the subject of the Congo army, moved in due course to the Middle East, and intervenes in the awkward matter of troublesome Belgian resistance groups – averted when they are shipped to Britain for training. This achievement closely follows action taken by Powell, late in 1944, described in Chapter 8 of *Faces in My Time*. This volume of the memoirs shows that *The Military Philosophers* is the most autobiographical part of *Dance*, some of the military attachés with whom he worked closely 'corresponding' to fictional characters; although it also reminds us that the novel shows us an imaginary world.

David Pennistone is Jenkins's immediate superior during the time he works with the Poles, and a friend and ally in the administrative 'wars' throughout. He is among the most formidable and likeable soldiers in the three war-volumes, a man who satisfies Vigny's and Lyautey's requirements with style: 'Though absolutely dedicated to his duties with the Poles, he also liked getting as much amusement out of the job as possible' (1). It is characteristic of him to be angry and amused at the same time when he hears of the escape, from a British military prison, of the adventurous Szymanski – actually abetted by Sunny Farebrother's 'secret show'; an episode both disgraceful, in the official view (the cause of Sunny's temporary disgrace) and diverting as a good example of Poles having 'a bit of dash'. Pennistone and Jenkins share 'amusement' in every detail possessing human interest to be learned about their European colleagues. Some anecdotes recall the continent under Occupation – far from their committee rooms: after the fall of France one attaché, General Bobrowski, commandeered railway trains, set bren-guns on the locomotives, and brought two Polish brigades to a Channel port. Military minutiae are found equally intriguing: Corporal Curtis, Pennistone discovers, once read the whole of Grote's *History of Greece*; Bobrowski started his career as a *praporschik*, or ensign, in a Russian regiment; Kielkiewitz was 'an aspirant – always a favourite rank of mine – in the Austro-Hungarian cavalry'(1). Caring for such details, for themselves and not because mastery of detail is a means to power, is one mark of how Pennistone differs from Widmerpool, in many ways his opposite among the military philosophers. He is equally effective, however, in combating administrative opponents, crushing the War Office's most obstructive petty bureaucrat, Mr Blackhead, classified by Pennistone as 'a super-tchenovnik of the classical Russian novel', by a means beyond Widmerpool's ken: his sense of fun. Blackhead's minutes, which have 'the abstract quality of pure extension' (Pennistone's phrase), are a serious incumbrance, delaying action on many fronts. His three and a half pages on 'Polish Women's Corps: soap issue' are returned with the addition, '*Please amplify, D. Pennistone, Maj. G. S.*' (1). Jenkins wonders whether Blackhead will retain his sanity after this decisive defeat.

Widmerpool in the Cabinet Offices is a Military Assistant Secretary; with fourteen hours or more of hard work a day and an equivalent application of will-power, he can use this position to influence the conduct of the war – as Peter Templer says when he and Jenkins meet in a high-government-level, and therefore underground, committee room: Widmerpool's present domain. This character, already devoted more space than any other, was by now regarded by many reviewers as the single greatest achievement of the sequence. A reader is likely to feel, hearing in this novel of the deaths of Stringham and Templer (Barnby's death having been reported in the last lines of *The Soldier's Art*), that Widmerpool alone of those Jenkins knows is certain to survive the war, an indispensable figure stumbling at the centre of the dance. He is still developing, and so are Jenkins's powers of inspection. It is in this book that we sense a sharp reduction in the difference between the narrator and his younger self. This is partly because the rich layers of wartime life make earlier periods seem more remote, so that the Widmerpool known at school existed 'millennia' ago, and the first years in London are now a 'legendary' period for the Jenkins of the 1940s and for the narrator. It is partly because experience as a staff officer matures Jenkins rapidly in various ways of the world. Watching Widmerpool from this point on, the Jenkinses of now and then merge in a complicated mix of reactions which sometimes includes horror.

There is no need to repeat the diagnosis of egoistic will-power, because the earlier volumes have established the character so firmly; we can interpret Widmerpoolisms for ourselves. Colonel Widmerpool has extended his methods of self-projection, bullying and boasting with more sophistication. He sounds as stilted as ever, thanks to Powell's flair for creating, and Jenkins's for mocking, a phrase or tone which is even fractionally out of place. Ill-judged colloquialisms are a sign of his unawareness of how he sounds. He lacks, for example, the social skill to find the right context and voice inflection for a 'Pongo' – Navy term for a soldier – when asking a naval colleague to lunch. Jenkins is merciless to such errors: 'I wondered whether in the access of self-abasement that seemed to have overcome him, Widmerpool would make a similar suggestion to the airman, referring to himself as a "brown job"' (2). Elsewhere, he carefully records the officious language with which Widmerpool uses the pretext of 'security' to order an old friend peremptorily out of the room. The same verbal crudeness, so ingrained that it would be absurd to ask whether he is consciously rude, marks his pronouncements on more far-reaching matters. Jenkins is present when he comments on reports of the massacre of Polish officers at Katyn. In these speeches on 'the very regrettable manner' in which the Russians have behaved, 'almost certainly . . . the consequence of administrative inadequacy, rather than wilful indifference to human life and the dictates of compassion', Powell's writing has an Orwellian force. It is an art quite different from Orwell's, however, in having created this almost delightfully offensive character, ready now that political satire is wanted to act as a mouthpiece for the official British attitude, echoed by civil servants in this scene in Chapter 2, towards Stalin, 'our second most powerful Ally'.

What Widmerpool is 'like' remains mysterious, for all that has been said about the ego and the will – forces strong enough after all in many less disagreeable characters. His marriage, at the end of this volume, deepens the mystery. Pamela Flitton, Stringham's stunningly beautiful niece, already has an impressive tally of damage and destruction among the male characters: Prince Theodoric, Szymanski, Odo Stevens and Peter Templer are among those she has tormented. The idea that she is evil, or perhaps courting damnation, arises in the scene where she meets Mrs Erdleigh, the fortune-teller and former associate of Uncle Giles, during an air-raid. Whatever her occult powers, to be neither scorned nor too solemnly regarded, according to the narrator, Myra Erdleigh is a forceful enough personality to produce just the sort of bizarre drama Jenkins most enjoys reporting in detail, and his account of Widmerpool and Pam at an embassy party is also very entertaining. Why she should select Widmerpool as a victim worth marrying, or what Furies within his personality drive him to her, are dark matters which arouse curiosity about the postwar novels.

Returning to 'the University' in 1945 as a method of re-entry into literary life, Jenkins does research for a book on Robert Burton (1577–1640) and his *Anatomy of Melancholy* (1621), 'long a favourite' and a change from novel-writing. Burton's great work, which analysed 'all the Kindes, Causes, Symptomes, Prognostickes, and several cures' of the condition, might, he feels, have included a subsection on 'post-war melancholy', from which he is suffering. The purlieus of the University are laden with the melancholy of youth, however, and *Books Do Furnish a Room* (1971) is a novel that often looks backward, remembering characters, many now deceased, who suffered from species of the melancholy-madness that Burton anatomised. 'Rather a morbid subject' is the comment of the housemaster Le Bas, still at work, although very old, and acting as librarian when Jenkins revisits his school in the last chapter. 'What's your generation?' he demands, as though officiating at the Last Judgment, and 'what happened to the others?' Mention of the deaths of Stringham and Templer recalls how both were 'morbid cases' before they died, Templer, his second wife having become clinically insane, painfully withdrawn from life before he chose to go on his secret mission.

Two other contrasted types of melancholy belong to Erridge and Umfraville. The funeral of Alfred Tolland, Viscount Erridge, Earl of Warminster, Jenkins's brother-in-law, occupies the second chapter of this novel and assembles many established characters, including Umfraville. Known only distantly at school, Erridge was encountered in *At Lady Molly's* where Quiggin was trying to exploit, socially and financially, the leftist inclinations of this gloomiest of the sequence's noblemen. The funeral gives Jenkins an opportunity to anatomise Erridge, 'a subject for Burton if ever there was one' (1); a melancholy case, he decides, 'wholly uninterested in individuals, his absorption only in "causes"'. As an individual, he is an interesting example of this commonplace category because he is so unpredictable. 'Uncle Alfred' Tolland, a different melancholy type, who is incapable of finishing a sentence, concludes that 'Of course Erridge always did . . .'. The narrator seizes on this as a chance to ramify speculations, concluding, 'perhaps just "do the unexpected"'. Apparently tied to a life of studious celibacy in his shabby flat in the servants' quarters at Thrubworth Park, he suddenly sets off for China with Mona, Templer's ex-wife, whom he detaches from

Quiggin; but Mona, who turns up at the funeral, as the wife of an Air Vice-Marshal, reports on a wretched journey to Hong Kong with 'Alf' who abominated spending a farthing on drink. An habitual reader of books on the Soviet economy, Erridge used to turn, at times of depression, to bound volumes of *Chums* and *Boy's Own Paper* – 'his only vice'. In his unpredictability, maintained even in dying in his forties, he resembles Umfraville except that whatever course he has followed has been, apparently, joyless.

Dicky Umfraville is a man of strength and ability who has only ever 'pottered' in life. The 'boundless unreliability of horses' has left its melancholy mark on his face, in repose, but he is usually animated, a good talker and impersonator, attractive to Jenkins because completely at ease with himself and others, a master of 'lounging elegance', able to run a night-club or serve as Lieutenant-Colonel on the staff of the Military Government in Germany. A more vivid and successful version of Eustace Bromwich in *What's Become of Waring*, he resembles his prototype in marrying recklessly and often; his fifth and lasting attempt, 'a good bet', is with Lady Frederica Tolland. Under his gaiety in company is a sadness to which he occasionally alludes. Of his marriage with Lady Anne Stepney, in *At Lady Molly's*, he comments, '"She didn't like grown-up life – and who shall blame her?" He sighed. "I don't like it much myself," he said'(4). His blend of gloom and high spirits has something in common with Jenkins's nature, and the narrator relishes all opportunities to record his talk and ruminate on his inconsistencies. Perhaps his melancholy belongs to his generation, those neither entirely pre-1914 nor entirely postwar, who are obliged to live 'in two eras'. There are other possibilities.

Widmerpool, in parliament and soon in minor office in Attlee's government, is observed in relation to Pamela, for whose sex-life the narrator finds a good epithet in 'gladiatorial', and, equally out of his element, among literary figures, in connection with the magazine *Fission* brought out by the new publishing firm of Quiggin and Craggs. 'Books-do-furnish-a-room' Bagshaw, its editor, and X. Trapnel the novelist, its foremost reviewer, are among the new characters. Books Bagshaw's hobby is the politics of the far left, and he is intrigued by the difficulty of 'placing' Widmerpool, obviously, he insists, more than an honest 'Labour man'. Talking to Books or Widmerpool, or to the two political caterpillars Sillery and Short the civil servant, re-encountered at the University, Jenkins resumes his 1930s role of bemused political innocent. He is more at ease with old literati connected with *Fission*, including Mark Members, and with new ones, including Ada Leintwardine, novelist (*I Stopped at a Chemist's*) and literary manager, and Trapnel.

X. might have bewildered Burton. He baffles and infuriates Widmerpool, while offering Jenkins almost as much scope for ruminating as Widmerpool himself. The key to him, we are told, is General Conyers's theory of the 'personal myth', satisfying which, the General says, is all that really matters in life.[47] Trapnel's personal myth, or imaginary self-conception, is unusually rich. Among the arch-egoists, Trapnel is more amusing than most, although his unstoppable monologues, and his impersonations, can be socially 'dangerous', Jenkins thinks. It is his inner life which wins Jenkins, deterred when Bagshaw first introduces them by Trapnel's eccentric clothes and sword-stick. Trapnel is a role-player of so many parts, he decides, that 'in the manner of Burton – an interminable catalogue of types' is required. The catalogue, given early in Chapter 4, abounds in romantic contraries, and the only role consistently achieved in reality, the narrator observes in conclusion, is that of 'being poor', although offset in Trapnel's fantasies by being also very rich. A gifted sponger, he relieves Widmerpool at the *Fission* party of a pound; later he detaches Pamela, affording a scene of confrontation in Chapter 4 – Widmerpool out-talking the levelled sword-stick – worthy of Jenkins's mettle as narrator, the extreme romantic pitted against the most prosaic of injured husbands. Pamela, whose destruction of the manuscript of Trapnel's masterpiece destroys him too, remains useful to the novelist for her effect on other characters, but frustrating to the narrator's gift for interpreting people, perhaps because her stylish, affected, rude façade conceals misery rather than melancholy. To encapsulate her, Jenkins borrows a phrase from St John Clarke, finding a good one: she likes 'to try conclusions with the maelstrom' (40). But this verdict, in his own terms, is 'frivolous' and he is left for once, where she is concerned, at a loss for words which really tell.

Pamela continues to act as though one of the Furies rather than as a character interesting in herself, in *Temporary Kings* (1973). A new character, Russell Gwinnett, an American academic, wishes to meet her because he is writing a book about

Trapnel. Another, Louis Glober, an American film-producer, wants to marry her, and may be willing to give her a star's part in her version of the Trapnel novel she destroyed. She continues to torment Widmerpool. The narrator observes her and the goings-on she instigates in the holiday atmosphere – for the first two-thirds of the novel – of a literary conference in Venice where he and many other of the characters, some old friends and acquaintances, have gathered to enjoy themselves, as 'temporary kings'. Melancholy darkens this volume, however, more than the previous one: Death is 'in evidence all round', as Gwinnett, who likes to capitalise his favourite word, concludes; power is considered in its sexual aspect, and – an exercise in the macabre perhaps suited to the narrator's later middle-age – in relation to death.

'You'll live like a king', says Mark Members, conference organiser, although not attending, and Jenkins asks if he means like the king who must die in *The Golden Bough*: 'Death in Venice'? Meeting Gwinnett brings thoughts of Trapnel, whom Bagshaw, now a television producer, admired in his last days for his 'melancholy distinguished air', and who hoped to do a documentary 'about his failure in life'. Bagshaw on Trapnel is followed by the academic Malcolm Crowding's account of Trapnel's dropping dead after an heroic evening of standing free drinks in his favourite literary pub. Contemplating the difficulty of explaining Trapnel to Gwinnett, Jenkins reflects that the American's enigmatic personality complicates the problem. Gwinnett aims to make his biography 'objective', although that method is 'under fire' – this is 1958. *Temporary Kings*, more crowded with incident than previous novels, is even more insistent that people and their goings-on exist as other people perceive, and, above all, relate them.

Jenkins's narrative about Gwinnett's search for a narrative about Trapnel leads him to research Gwinnett, hearing about him from a former colleague and friend of the American, Dr Emily Brightman; a scholar about whom there is no 'spinsterish prudery' or 'academic fussiness'. Gwinnett is afflicted by a sort of seventeenth-century, or possibly romantic, love-in-death melancholy – something, Brightman and Jenkins agree, not in the American tradition. The Widmerpools are in Venice as guests of Jacky Bragadin, whose palace contains Tiepolo's ceiling of *Candaules and Gyges*, a treatment of the myth in which King Candaules allows his friend Gyges to view his wife naked. Pamela is excited by this painting, perhaps because the queen resembles her – as Jenkins thinks, relying on Trapnel's report – in being frigid yet sexually insatiable, perhaps because of the story that, considering herself to have been raped by the visual possession, the queen causes Gyges to kill her husband and take his place. One result is that Pamela goes on the offensive, at a meeting with Gwinnett in the Basilica of San Marco, as he reports to Jenkins.

'She grabbed hold of me,' he said.
'You mean – '
'Just that – '
'By the balls?'
'Yeah.'
'Literally?'
'Quite literally. Then she hinted the story about Ferrand-Sénéschal was true.' (3)

Jenkins has never lagged behind literary fashion; as a narrator of 1973, he manages such frankness with aplomb, and follows with his usual assiduity the details of what now develops into Pamela's hunt for Gwinnett, who is obliged, for the sake of his biography, to enter 'the Trapnel world' of shabby pubs and hotels. Back in London, she presents herself naked at midnight in Bagshaw's house, where Gwinnett is lodging, an episode to be reconstructed by the narrator, and finally dies by an overdose so that Gwinnett can enjoy, it seems, he being a necrophiliac, her ultimate sacrifice. Ferrand-Sénéschal is a French Marxist intellectual who has died in a Kensington hotel in cirumstances, treated as scandalous by the French popular press, involving the Widmerpools. It later appears that the Frenchman died in bed with Pamela during a scene staged for the voyeurist pleasure of Widmerpool. Moreland, given the last word on this affair, attributes it to 'the love of power that makes the true voyeur'.

Now a Life Peer, Widmerpool is threatened by political as well as by sexual scandal, and here again the lengths to which a lust for power can take him are mystifying to the narrator. Lord Widmerpool's visit to Venice includes an unsuccessful attempt to see his eastern European 'contact', Dr Belkin, an old Communist hard-liner who later denounces him in the course of state trials in his (once Theodoric's) country. According to Pamela, her husband saves himself from prison by betraying all he knows about Ferrand-Sénéchal's activities. His motive for having taken such risks is obscure: it appears that he has made a fortune out of Balkan wines. Bagshaw, speaking as an expert, tells Jenkins that being a 'crypto' is often satisfying to a taste for power. He and Jenkins agree that Widmerpool is 'the greatest bourgeois who ever lived' (1), but Bagshaw insists that this need be no obstacle to espionage and treason, given a strong and possibly wounded ego. The war-novels imply that Widmerpool might have been happier administering the Nazi party, and this novel implies that, in different circumstances, he might have flourished for a while under Stalin. Powell's view that left-wing politics attract humourless egotists appears again in Dan Tokenhouse, visited in Venice, a caricature of an untalented Marxist painter ('Four priests rigging a miracle'). Jenkins's interest in him, and amusement at his pleasure in the rare event of selling a picture, make him seem human, burdened by his obsessions, living in a weird private world we can imagine only from knowing something of its melancholy. He might remind us of the narrator's 'eminently Burtonesque' reverie on page 3 of *Books Do Furnish a Room*, about the many persons once known – Tokenhouse was Jenkins's father's friend – 'now dead, gone off their rocker, withdrawn into states of existence they – or I – had no wish to share'. There is a different sort of melancholy, and an emphatic contrast between the man of power and the civilised man, in the last pages of this volume where the dying Moreland retains to the end his lively interest in books and people. Leaving Moreland for the last time, at the close of *Temporary Kings*, Jenkins meets Widmerpool apparently 'unhinged' by misfortunes. As they talk a rally of vintage cars passes along the Embankment, symbols, mournful and amusing, of the passage of time, all but invisible to Widmerpool, however, who (in the final verdict of this novel) 'was never greatly interested in other people's doings'.

Hearing Secret Harmonies (1975) ends the sequence with the sharpest possible contrast between the serenity of the narrator and the wretched decline and fall of Widmerpool. Jenkins meets all the characters from earlier volumes who are still alive, adds memories of many others, and gets to know a few newcomers. The Furies drive Widmerpool, at least half-mad, to his death, in scenes combining horror with comedy as boldly as any in modern fiction. These too involve, as we expect, figures from the past.

Sir Magnus Donners is long dead, but his widow Matilda presides over the literary prize which commemorates his name and she persuades Jenkins to join Mark Members, an 'almost statutory' member of any arts committee, and Dame Emily Brightman, still talking about 'that poor little Lady Widmerpool' and 'her naughtinesses' (2), in judging the latest entries. At Matilda's flat he meets Norman Chandler, to whom Mrs Foxe was long enslaved, now directing the new play in which Polly Duport, daughter of Jean (Templer), is to be the star. This is a good opportunity for nostalgia, and Nick needs only the slightest pretext. Soon after reporting these meetings he recalls the last time he saw Sunny Farebrother, travelling home on the tube from the funeral of Jimmy Stripling, and learned, fifty years after the event, that Sunny was aware of the practical joke Jimmy tried on him in vain at the Templer's, as described in *A Question of Upbringing*. The disclosure of such final details is another of the melancholy pleasures of this volume. Later there is a family wedding at Stourwater Castle, long a girls' school – its pupils perhaps raising the ghost of Sir Magnus, Jenkins fancies – and Dicky Umfraville, at eighty, Hugo Tolland and Flavia Wisebite, Stringham's sister and Pamela's mother, are there, more or less agreeably remembering things past, until Widmerpool arrives.

Chancellor of one of the new universities and, since his travels in the United States, a champion of youth and the alternative society, Ken Widmerpool, his title disdained as a trapping of the false 'bourgeois' society he now 'rejects', is sometimes to be seen on television. At the end of a programme about St John Clarke, Quiggin and Members speculating freely on the subject of Clarke's queer sexual tastes, the Jenkinses stay for the news and see the Chancellor, processing in full regalia, showered with red paint by girls who turn out to be the Quiggin twins (J. G. having married Ada Leintwardine). He appears to be highly excited, reminding Jenkins of the incident of Barbara Goring and the sugar. Since Widmerpool is a trustee of the Magnus Donners Prize, the committee are anxious, when they have chosen Gwinnett's biography of Trapnel, *Death's-head Swordsman*, for this year's award, lest he oppose their choice; they are relieved to learn that he does not care what Gwinnett has written about him. As he explains in his speech at the prize-giving, he is now a champion of 'contemporary counterculture'. This means that he is opposed to all traditional writing and to all traditions: 'to what is – or rather was – absurdly called honour, respectability, law, order, obedience, custom, rule, hierarchy, precept, regulation' – and many other such false pretences (3). Amanda and Belinda Quiggin have taught him to acknowledge the necessity of violent protest: 'Even now there are marks of red paint on my body, that may remain until my dying day, as memorial to a weak spirit.' At this point the twins, whom he has brought to the dinner as his guests, release the stink-bombs they have brought with them.

The next of the novel's social occasions is a Royal Academy dinner where Jenkins sits next to Canon Paul Fenneau, a character retrieved from the diffident undergraduate called 'Paul' at Sillery's tea-parties (mentioned three times in *A Question of Upbringing*). Fenneau, a sleek, fashionable London cleric, erudite in occult matters, tells the story of Scorp Murtlock, the charismatic, sinister young man Jenkins has met already, leading a small group of disciples in pursuit of 'Harmony' by magic and meditation. Widmerpool introduces himself to the canon, begging to be put in touch with Murtlock; despite a portentous warning from Fenneau, he joins the 'commune'. Jenkins is interested in the group because Isobel's niece Fiona Cutts belongs. He learns more of it because Gwinnett, working on gothic themes in Jacobean drama, undertakes 'research' on the nocturnal rites by means of which Murtlock attempts to raise the spirit of Dr Trelawney. A new friend, Gibson Delavacquerie, a poet-businessman, rescues Fiona and provides further information. The relationship of mutual attraction and hostility between Murtlock and Widmerpool is, we gather, a power-struggle which Widmerpool is losing. When the Stourwater wedding-party is invaded by the blue-robed children of Harmony, he is grotesquely subject to the bizarre rule of the cult and its leader's perhaps sadistic whims. He is also physically exhausted – cross-country running, by night and in the nude, being part of the system – and mentally unbalanced. Jenkins finds him, none the less, as much as ever a figure of fun. Present at the wedding is Sir Bertram Akworth, another very minor figure from the first volume; Widmerpool caused him, there, to be 'sacked' from school for sending a love-note to Peter Templer; hoping to restore Harmony, he now falls on his knees, grovelling before Akworth. What might have been a dramatic climax, more pointed since he and Akworth have been rivals in the City, is a failure: people assume, as at first does the narrator, that he is searching for something he has dropped on the floor. It is Bithel, for many of the postwar years a tramp and alcoholic, now a creature of Murtlock's, who brings the news on the last pages of the novel, of Widmerpool's having died on a night-time run, defying Harmony by trying to run faster than the rest. Our last direct view of him is more memorable, funny and pathetic, and in keeping both with his character and the narrator's puzzled appraisal of him: after the failure of his penance before Akworth, he is seen 'haranguing' the group, perhaps explaining the significance of his abasement, Jenkins thinks, perhaps just organising the run back to base.

The title phrase is from the seventeenth-century poet, Thomas Vaughan, invoked by Mrs Erdleigh: she had spoken, the narrator remembers, of how 'the liberated soul ascends, looking at the sunset, and hearing secret harmonies', and he thinks this may explain why the girls in Murtlock's group have 'Harmony' on their T-shirts. The beauty of Vaughan's words is such a contrast to the squalid rites performed in Harmony's service, however – 'negative' sexual acts within the charmed circle and so forth – that the title applies only ironically to such goings-on. Mrs Erdleigh, who used to 'put out' the cards for Uncle Giles, or supervise planchette – upsetting the sceptical Quiggin with a surprising session at the Templers' house in *The Acceptance World* – and her male counterpart Trelawney are milder figures than Murtlock, although it is implied that their activities possess unpleasant sides. Jenkins's moderate view, that 'mumbo-jumbo' is not completely to be dismissed, its practitioners not to be taken too solemnly either, is most actively challenged in this last volume, which links power with sorcery, and hints at evil forces, from an unseen psychic universe, which might explain the patterns of the dance. Coincidence is 'magic in action', Jenkins recalls Trelawney having said (1). Fenneau tells him that 'To those familiar with the rhythm of living there are few surprises in this world' (4). He also says that much must remain 'unrevealed', and although Jenkins's sense of fun prevents him from taking pronouncements of this kind too seriously, there are frequent hints that they cannot be completely laughed away. If Jenkins were asked for last thoughts about life, he might quote Delavacquerie: 'Love and Literature should rank before Sorcery and Power' (5). But lecturing on 'significance' is Widmerpool's characteristic role, not Jenkins's.

Widmerpool's assertions of the first volume, about how 'it doesn't do to read too much', and certainly not 'trash from modern novels', finally seem to have been narrated and laughed away, with a remarkable lightness of touch, in the last volume, in the management of so many strands in so long a story. The sequence attacks his values in other ways. The liveliness of the dialogue is one of its great pleasures: Widmerpool is out-talked in every volume by scores of witty, entertaining speakers. Even more effective, and further from Widmerpool's ken, is the poetical realm of the fiction, or, in a term Jenkins favours, its mythology.

4

A Dance to the Music of Time: Myth

'Myth' is the narrator's term for stories told and retold with imagination, to oneself and to like-minded friends. He explains that Moreland's aunt has a prominent place in his 'personal mythology', and that General Conyers has his place in Jenkins's 'family myth'.[48] The more imaginative the telling, the more mythical the stories become; but retelling is another essential feature. Jenkins's myths use motifs and images drawn from paintings, buildings, costumes and other elements of the background of the action that occupy the foreground of the narrative. They often cause delays and digressions but also create interconnections in the larger design. The effect is to enrich the human interest and also to involve figurative writing so expressive and complex that the sequence can be thought of as a comic epic in the poetic sense, as well as in being a long and grandly conceived work of fiction.

An example of a background detail which achieves a place in the foreground because it grows into a sort of myth is Mr Deacon's painting, *Boyhood of Cyrus*, introduced in the first chapter of *A Buyer's Market*. The next chronological stage of Jenkins's career, and the intended subject of the chapter, is his love and pursuit of Barbara Goring in early London days; but Barbara is approached very indirectly. The volume opens with memories of a sale-room inspected twenty years later (as we learn in *Hearing Secret Harmonies*). Several of Mr Deacon's canvases were auctioned there and sold for a few pounds. That leads to childhood memories of the painter and of a meeting in the Louvre during a family holiday six or seven years before the era of Barbara Goring. The point of this preamble (in itself a lively and amusing character portrait), we gather, is that 'a Deacon', *Boyhood of Cyrus*, formerly hung in the hall of the Walpole-Wilsons' house in Eaton Square. It was here that Jenkins used to see Barbara, so that while the picture at first summoned up recollections of childhood, it soon developed a further 'mystic significance' as the 'symbol' of Barbara's presence, or at least of the two-to-one chance of her being present.

Powell derives various kinds of fun from these, perhaps Proustian, associations of ideas. The picture's incongruity as a symbol of early love is made more funny by assurances of how bad it is as a work of art. No opportunity is lost for emphasising the worthlessness, in Jenkins's opinion, of all Mr Deacon's pictures. Weakly drawn, they are reckless in their use of colour. *Boyhood of Cyrus* is more acceptable than most of the others because it is relatively small. One vast panorama of ancient Greek runners, which chanced to be placed upside-down in the sale-room, was perhaps to be viewed 'at greater advantage in that reversed position'. If Mr Deacon's work can be thought of in terms of cultural background, the narrator reflects, it derives from Victorian Hellenism and might therefore be compared 'although at a greatly inferior level of the imagination's faculties, with Le Bas's daydreams of Hellas'. Barbara still waits, pages ahead. The comedy benefits from the narrator's refusal to be hurried in the course of his wandering logic. Le Bas used to talk about 'the blue Sicilian sea' of the ancient world – and no such analogy is ever to be left unnoticed – but it would be unfair to impugn the quality of his imagination by comparing it, even remotely, with Mr Deacon's. 'Daydreams', the slightest possible term for Le Bas's superior creative achievement, is typical of Powell's relentless quest for the utmost limit to a line of comic speculation. *Boyhood of Cyrus* is precious in Jenkins's memory because the picture is soaked in the delight and anguish of love for Barbara, but no trace of any other kind of respect for it must remain unobliterated. Insisting on how bad the pictures are assists another aspect of the comedy, the point that their classical status veils the fact that they sell mostly to homosexuals. Jenkins's parents, who used to comment ironically on Mr Deacon's claim that he preferred to keep his canvases rather than sell them, were unaware that businessmen sometimes travelled from as far as Lancashire to buy male nudes such as *Antinous* or *Spartan youth at exercise*. The scene in *Boyhood of Cyrus* is not described in *A Buyer's Market* but its impact is implied by Eleanor Walpole-Wilson's reactions:

'Are they going bathing? I don't like it'.

The narrator dwells just as emphatically on the picture's power over his mind, at the time of his passion for Barbara and afterwards, as on its poor quality and unseemly content, wringing amusement from the unrelatedness of passion to picture. The magic spell, unknown to Mr Deacon or to Barbara (who has never noticed the picture), is comic in itself. Any classical scene glimpsed in a dealer's window, Jenkins confesses, would remind him of *Boyhood of Cyrus* and therefore of Barbara. Overhearing the name Cyrus, even years afterwards, would recall 'the pains of early love'. The obstruction of the story of Barbara is also entertaining. The narrator takes advantage of every opening which leads away from her and lets him exploit the subject of the painting instead, remarking, for example, that 'fortunately' Cyrus's name does not often occur in conversation.

Order is restored to the narrative after these digressions, by coincidence. Such are the movements of the Dance that when Barbara has killed Jenkins's love by pouring sugar over Widmerpool, he meets Mr Deacon, attended by his assistant Gypsy Jones, in the street outside, and Stringham takes them, with Widmerpool, to Milly Andriadis's party. Jenkins is delighted to be able to say that he has seen Cyrus this evening, and he is impressed when the artist guesses that it is ignobly 'skyed' in the hall. Coincidence makes another link with the painting and its spell because in the last pages of *A Buyer's Market*, in Mr Deacon's shop on the evening of the day of his funeral, Jenkins and Gypsy Jones make love, completing an ironic design begun in the first chapter.

Boyhood of Cyrus is now so firmly established in Jenkins's mind that whenever in later volumes he thinks of Barbara, or early love, or 'deb' dances, or bad art, he is always liable to remember it, or some other Deacon. Meeting Sir Gavin Walpole-Wilson at the memorial exhibition of another bad painter, Horace Isbister, RA, in *The Acceptance World*, Jenkins reminds him of Cyrus. They agree that its first owner, Sir Gavin's father-in-law Lord Aberavon, whose portrait was painted by Isbister, was 'not a man of taste' (4). Pillars and marble decorations in a bar, in *At Lady Molly's*, recall Mr Deacon's pictures, perhaps *Pupils of Socrates*, since these designs are obviously the work of 'someone who had also brooded long and fruitlessly on classical themes' (4). When Gwatkin mentions 'the great Lord Aberavon' in *The Valley of Bones*, Jenkins thinks of *Boyhood of Cyrus* and of his love for Barbara 'in prehistoric times'. He argues that Gwatkin is distantly related to Aberavon, eager to extend the picture's mythical ramifications in a new direction, one almost boundless since that family goes back to Hengist and Horsa, but Gwatkin's imagination is not equal to these flights (4).

We learn on the first page of *Hearing Secret Harmonies* that the hanging gardens of Babylon could be seen in *Boyhood of Cyrus*, as a background to a group of 'woodenly posed' youths. The gardens are brought to mind by comparison with the storeyed platforms of a cliff in a quarry near Jenkins's home, seen through mist. Physically engaged in catching crayfish with Scorpio Murtlock and disciples, he is transported back in memory to the shadows of the Walpole-Wilsons' hall, forty years before. In the last chapter of the novel and in one of the last scenes of the sequence, he visits the 'Bosworth Deacon Centenary Exhibition'. This is 'not so much a Resurrection as a Second Coming' (7): cleaned and restored, and lauded in the press ('sadomasochistic broodings in paint'), the pictures are selling briskly, *Boyhood of Cyrus* already tagged. E. Bosworth Deacon was Edgar to his own circle; Jenkins has always retained 'Mr'; 'Bosworth' is the invention of Barnabas Henderson's gallery: 'a remarkable artist'. Being a Man of Taste, Jenkins would not have bought *Cyrus*, but there is a sense in which it belongs to him, and it is fitting, funny and melancholy that we should take an almost final view of him pondering this icon of his youth and discovering in its background not only Babylon and his local quarries but also, though he cannot persuade Henderson, bored by the 'extraneous imagery' of pictures, to agree, Battersea Power Station.

Cyrus enters the narrator's world by a sort of metonymy: it is an adjunct of Barbara. *The Seven Deadly Sins* are symbolic and allegorical in both their states, as sixteenth-century tapestries and as photographs taken by Sir Magnus Donners. Jenkins shares their meanings with other characters but it is he who scrutinises them most exhaustively and he alone fully grasps their significance. The tapestries, perhaps Gobelins, are found in the drawing-room at Stourwater Castle, on the first visit, with Sir Gavin's party, in *A Buyer's Market*. Jenkins sits next to *Luxuria*, Lust. A figure composed of wings, horns, roses and naked breasts, attended by a Cupid and a goat, she is drawn in her car by a seven-headed Apocalyptic beast. There are bedroom scenes in the background. His neighbour is Templer's sister Jean Duport, who surprises and excites him by the liveliness with which she is able to discuss the details and extraneous imagery of this spectacle. *Luxuria* romanticises their meeting and the affair which follows in the next volume; it also lightly implies a judgment. Jenkins has already begun to turn the picture into literature when he meets Jean: Hercules watches Luxuria's progress gloomily, 'his mind filled, no doubt, with disquieting recollections' (3). Jean updates the scene. The devil or satyr who is 'lending a hand' in one of the bedrooms is the sort of friend of the family every newly married couple needs, she says. His immediate reaction is to think that he can have been in love with Barbara only 'amateurishly'. It is only gradually, in the course of many volumes, that he learns the extent to which Jean, mistress of Jimmy Brent as well as Jimmy Stripling, and even as Madame Flores ready 'to tromp' the elegant Dictator 'with the gauchos', is a worthy present-day daughter of Luxuria.

Diminished in grandeur when revisited ten years later in *The Kindly Ones*, the castle still has something of the air of a palace of lust, hinting at the unusual sins of its owner. Barnby's nude of the waitress from Casanova's Chinese Restaurant hangs near a statuette of *Cupid Chastised*. The tapestries have retained, even expanded their appeal, however, and they again 'engulf' Jenkins's imagination (2). It is inevitable, therefore, that when the guests agree to pose after dinner for Sir Magnus's camera, Moreland putting forward Rubens's *Rape of the Sabine Women* and other good ideas for tableaux, that Jenkins should think of doing modern variations on the sins that are, imaginatively speaking, his property. Each actor depicts his or her sin before the appropriate tapestry, so that *Luxuria* is the backcloth for Peter Templer's 'Three Ages of Lust'. In the last Age, Lady Anne Stepney (temporarily Umfraville) plays ballet girl to Templer's lustful octogenarian. This provokes an hysterical breakdown on the part of the latest Mrs Templer, the feeble-witted, neurotic Betty, already pushed to the brink of insanity by Templer's philandering, and informed of his current affair with Anne. It is not until he next meets Templer, in *The Military Philosophers*, that Jenkins learns of Betty's fate: 'off her rocker' and 'in the bin' (1). Shaken by his wife's madness, Templer has 'given up girls', and has little appetite left for life. After a last unhappy affair, with Pamela, he dies on a commando mission. In Jenkins's mythology, his story is as closely connected, therefore, with the photographs of lust as his sister's has been with *Luxuria*.

Thirty years after the night the photographs were taken, Matilda bribes Jenkins to join the Magnus Donners Prize Committee with a promise of a view of them, and it is unsurprising that these relics of a bygone age prove 'as irresistible as the Sins themselves' (*Hearing Secret Harmonies, 2*). Norman Chandler is also asked to the private view because the sins are 'his period'; and he tries to give them what would be a new lease of narrative life by linking them with the prize, to be given, he proposes, to the book which 'best enhances the Sin of the Year'. Jenkins searches for other connections in the past. Moreland's Gluttony, sprawled over an upturned fruitbowl and spilt glass of Kummel, recalls how Mopsy Pontner was 'done' by Louis Glober on the dining-table of his Mayfair hotel, forty years before. Two liqueur glasses, Mopsy told him at the time, were broken on that occasion. When Moreland himself, already gravely ill, in *Temporary Kings*, was reminded of that story, he was so alarmingly rocked by laughter that he forecast his death and started composing his obituary under the heading, 'Musician Dies from Nostalgia' (5). Another line of thought leads to Sir Magnus. Were his voyeuristic leanings encouraged by photographing the Sins, and did he introduce Widmerpool to such 'practices'? Matilda makes a contribution of her own to the mythology of the Sins. Widmerpool, who interrupted the charades by marching in wearing uniform (the year was 1938), ought to have represented the eighth sin, Humbug.

Later in *Hearing Secret Harmonies*, when Jenkins is invited to the Sebastian Cutts–Clare Akworth wedding at Stourwater, he accepts because he hopes to revisit the past. The school authorities have removed the tapestries, of course, and substituted Annigoni's portrait of the Queen. They remain visible to the mind's eye, and Jenkins is occupied in reconstructing his meeting with Jean, and 'the great impersonation of the Sins', when the newly married Gwinnett and Fiona Cutts come into the room. It is useless, he finds, to try to pass the myth on to them. Jean will reappear later in the book, not here but among the Deacons, and transformed into a great South American lady. The Jean of memory and *Luxuria* belongs to a bygone age.

Other visual images of mythical force are indebted to a style, school or period, rather than to a particular picture. At the Conyers's, in *At Lady Molly's*, a photograph of the General wearing the uniform of a Gentleman at Arms and carrying a halberd emerges from the background of the scene because the details are remembered from a visit during childhood. Mrs Conyers explains that the General is at cello practice. Jenkins 'cannot help imagining him' as a military cellist in a Dutch genre painting, the uniform and the halberd (propped against the wall) transferred into the painting from the photograph (2). The Dutch style is suitably attractive and also aptly impressive because of 'the deep social conviction' of the painters, matching the General's perfect assurance. His social ease derives in part from the 'dim archaic period', 'remote and legendary', in which Conyers first knew Jenkins's parents and won his place in 'family myth'. It is partly Conyers's personal achievement, iconographically rendered in the narrative by an imaginative painting in a traditionally civilised manner. Such imagery does not, of course, conflict with the General's often startlingly avant-garde opinions and up-to-date behaviour.

Early observation of Le Bas may have taught Jenkins his habit of verbal cartooning. Descriptions of the housemaster in *A Question of Upbringing* dwell on his odd postures, animal images reflecting his pupils' enjoyment of the idea of his ungainliness: 'he crouched there in the manner of a large animal – some beast alien to the English countryside, a yak or sea-lion – taking its ease: marring, as Stringham said later, the beauty of the summer afternoon' (1). The narrator finds pictorial equivalents: Le Bas is inclined to pose 'like an athlete or ballet-dancer' and to balance, feet turned in the same direction, on the fender, postures lending 'the air of belonging to some highly conventionalised form of graphic art: an oriental god or knave of playing cards' (1). Later in the volume, on a visit to the university, Le Bas holds his hands up parallel 'like an Egyptian god, or figure from the Bayeux tapestry' (4). Before he meets Milly Andriadis, Jenkins expects, perhaps because her name is Greek, that she will be akin to Le Bas in resembling a 'formalised classical figure from bronze or ceramic art'. In the artist's model Mona a very different effect is achieved by the same sort of appeal to a style of sculpture; she is 'like a strapping statue of Venus conceived at a period when more than a touch of vulgarity had found its way into classical sculpture'. That is in *At Lady Molly's* (3), but the narrator is always inclined to remember Mona in sculptural images, with an implication present also in the depictions of Le Bas that the character (gender being as irrelevant here as in the mutability achieved through will-power by Sillery and Miss Weedon) is hard to imagine in human terms.

One of the best examples of this literary caricature raised to the level of myth-making is in *The Soldier's Art*. General Liddament, at table in his mess, and his two full colonels, Hogbourne-Johnson and Pedlar, are transfigured into an ancient Egyptian sculpted trinity. The scene has been prepared by earlier passages which provide animal equivalents for the facial expressions of the colonels. Hogbourne-Johnson, fat and beaky-nosed, resembles an owl, 'an angry ageing bird, recently baulked of a field-mouse'. Colonel Pedlar is like a hound, faithful but 'not in the top class for picking up a difficult scent'. An oil-lamp in the mess unifies the three senior officers' heads: 'The faces of the two colonels, bird and beast, added a note deliberately grotesque, surrealist, possibly indicating a satirical meaning on the part of the artist, a political cartoonist, perhaps.' Pondering General Liddament's ascetic, schoolmasterly or priestly features, Jenkins grasps the appropriate artistic medium.

> Here was Pharaoh, carved in the niche of a shrine between two tutelary deities, who shielded him from human approach. All was manifest. Colonel Hogbourne-Johnson and Colonel Pedlar were animal-headed gods of Ancient Egypt. Colonel Hogbourne-Johnson was, of course, Horus, one of those sculptured representations in which the Lord of the Morning Sun resembles an owl rather than a falcon; a bad-tempered owl at that. Colonel Pedlar's dog's muzzle, on the other hand, was a milder version of jackal-faced Anubis, whose dominion over Tombs and the Dead did indeed fall within A. and Q.'s province. (1)

Extended metaphor is inserted here into a scene where the dialogue, entertaining to read, reflects that of British army messes at their most stupefyingly boring, and it represents a rebellion on Jenkins's part against the inanity of the colonels, a refusal to live with them, mentally, as they actually are. The verbal cartooning is aggressive. A typically Powellian device is the intensifying of attack with a show of fairness: Pedlar's looks are 'milder' than those of jackal-faced Anubis – although Hogbourne-Johnson's expression compensates for that shortcoming in the analogy.

The last touch of fancy about A. and Q. (Administration and Quartermaster) is far-fetched, but the 'shielding' of Pharaoh neatly fits the usual army joke about generals' godlike status. Imaginative rendering of the other members of the mess extends the attack to the despicably obsequious Cocksidge: 'certainly the lowest of slaves, cleaning out with his hands the priest's latrine, if such existed on the temple's premises'. Henceforth the colonels can be transformed at any moment into their poetic equivalents. Jenkins sees in Finn 'an enormous bird', but one 'immensely more powerful than Hogbourne-Johnson, an Egyptian deity belonging to a lower order of being than an officer of Finn's calibre'.

These pictures belong to a private 'mythology' which narrator and reader share. Their appeal derives from the way they recur. Their reappearances strengthen the illusions on which the story-telling depends: that we know Jenkins's past and can remember Barnby laughing over 'Edgar' long ago, that we understand the meaning of *Cyrus* and the Sins in ways that Henderson and Matilda cannot guess, that we have enjoyed a joke beyond the colonels' ken, and that we too can hear the secret harmonies. *Candaules and Gyges*, Jacky Bragadin's 'Tiepolo', in *Temporary Kings* has a different function. All the characters who see it have views on how it ought to be interpreted. Emily Brightman lectures on it as classical history, perhaps legend, or myth in the conventional sense. Pamela can see that Candaules might represent Widmerpool and the chamber in his palace the London hotel bedroom where Ferrand-Sénéschal died in bed with her; alternatively that the picture might illustrate the tastes of Sir Magnus Donners. *Candaules* makes a good subject for copious and entertaining talk: Dr Brightman is still exploring facets of it in the next volume. It also launches the strange affair of Pamela and Gwinnett. It only becomes absorbed into Jenkins's mythology, however, by association with two other pictures, artistically humbler, but more potent in his imagination.

As he walks with Gwinnett through the *calles* to the Bragadin Palace, mention of Glober transports Jenkins to the 1920s and his job with the publishing firm. Daniel Tokenhouse was closeted with St John Clarke, haggling over the fee for the never-to-be-written introduction to *The Art of Horace Isbister*, when Glober called. Ante-room conversation turned to Augustus John and Glober's wish to buy a drawing. Jenkins knew that Mopsy

Pontner's husband had a John for sale. By and by, he and Glober talk of Mopsy, under the Tiepolo. The drawing that Glober bought was of Conchita, a model of Barnby's, whose oil-sketch of her hung at Stourwater not far from the Sins: not the waitress from Casanova's but the girl whom Moreland used to call 'antithesis of the pavement artist's . . . loaf of bread, captioned *Easy to Draw but Hard to Get*'. Mopsy Pontner and Conchita contrast with Candaules's haughty ruthless queen pictured naked on the ceiling, and thoughts of them, as Glober reminisces, lead back from the scene of ancient misconduct, which now appears so up to date, to the 'pre-historic' times when Moreland and Barnby used to sit in the Mortimer talking about the ways of women.

Far below the level of artistic achievement represented by Barnby and Augustus John, inferior, perhaps even to the work of Mr Deacon, certainly lacking his 'self-conscious professionalism' (*Temporary Kings*, 1), are the paintings of Daniel Tokenhouse. Jenkins gallantly struggles to praise *Four Priests Rigging a Miracle*, but he is too bourgeois in his conceptions of art to grasp its revolutionary commitment, and he sees only its browns, greys and blacks. It is when Glober buys, for his collection of twentieth-century primitives, what he takes to be *The Emigrant Ship* but is actually a picture of 'a poor family found travelling without a ticket on the vaporetto' that Tiepolo's name arises. Such coincidences are, of course, reminders of Time's music, but this one is very plausible. Struggling to parcel the canvas with copies of *Unità* and string, Tokenhouse remarks that 'the patrons of Veronese or Tiepolo would need more than the painter's morning paper to bring their purchases home wrapped up'. The old man's pleasure in the first genuine sale of his career, and his rare joke, entitle him, for a moment, to kinship with the masters of his art: he is a painter too, and, by his criterion, a more 'progressive' one. The idea of the contrast between the murky gloom of a Tokenhouse and the glorious colour of Jacky Bragadin's ceiling suddenly makes us believe in the Tiepolo Powell has invented, and draws it into the mythology of *Dance*. It also reminds us how crucial comedy is to his myth-making. Widmerpool, baffled by all paintings because he never looks at them, cannot tell a Tokenhouse from a Tiepolo (3).

The sequence teems with references to pictures and other works of art, fictional or not. Characters are often linked with pictures or artists. Moreland's looks are those of a Bronzino portrait.

Stringham as a boy resembles, although slighter, Alexander, possibly Hephaistion, in Veronese's picture of Alexander receiving the children of Darius after the Battle of Issus.[49] If that precise identification were rejected, comparison could not be denied with young men in ruffs in portraits of that period. Mark Members is linked with Millais's *The Boyhood of Raleigh* because he assumes the posture of Raleigh in that picture (sitting clutching his knees) in Sillery's sitting-room when an undergraduate, later throwing himself on the floor like the Dying Gladiator. Fictional *objets d'art* tend to lodge more firmly in the narrator's memory and so to recur more effectively, making dance-like connections in the narrative, when they are artistically poor. The statuette, a small bronze, of *Truth Unveiled by Time*, makes its first appearance in the Mortimer where Norman Chandler sells it to Mr Deacon, shortly before the painter's death, recovering it later from the shop so that it can appear under the Romney in Mrs Foxe's drawing-room in *Casanova's Chinese Restaurant* (1, 3), to be regarded with contempt in due course by Lord Huntercombe. In the last chapter of *Hearing Secret Harmonies*, Chandler asks Jenkins if he remembers when the statuette was sold to Mr Deacon. Its name reflects with a pleasantly light touch on the sequence's title-theme.

Other pictures are remembered in association with houses, their comings and goings marking changes of fortune, or simply the passage of time, establishing further links among the volumes and reaffirming thoughts of the Dance. Lady Molly's pictures convey the nature of the blitz on London, in which she and Priscilla Lovel are killed when her house is hit, in *The Soldier's Art*. After the bombing, Jenkins looks at the discoloured patches on the walls where the Richard Wilson and the Greuze, removed for safety, hung when he first called with Chips (killed in the same raid) in *At Lady Molly's*, and that the Moroccan pastels, which remain, have been disturbed by the impact, the glass splintered on *Rainy Day at Marrakesh*. Many more extended and dramatic accounts of the effects of war in modern literature have less immediacy and sadness. The seascapes to be seen in the final chapter (with the Deacon exhibition) in Henderson's gallery, were last inspected in Peter Templer's house on the occasion in *The Acceptance World* when Planchette warned Quiggin that Mark Members was about to win back the St John Clarke secretaryship. With them then was the 'terrible' Isbister portrait of

Templer's father, on which 'a whole Marxist sermon might be preached', which takes us back to his house by the sea in *A Question of Upbringing*, 'a residence torn by some occult power from more appropriate suburban setting, and, at the same time, much magnified' (2). There it was the only painting. When Bithel brings Stringham's Modigliani to Henderson at the very end of *Dance*, rescued from Widmerpool's funeral pyre, it leads back by way of Trapnel's lair in Maida Vale where it hung among the red parrots and blue storks ('freak birds of the same size') of the wallpaper, and Widmerpool's cheerless apartment in Victoria Street, to Stringham's flat, where Widmerpool put him to bed, drunk, on the night of the Le Bas dinner. Amidst so much bad art in the last pages, its survival is fitting, its beautiful lines a triumph over all Henderson's Deacons, and it puts Widmerpool finally in his place because of his remark about it, that he could never remember the artist's name.

Places can have 'mythical significance', especially those frequently called to mind by association with other elements of the Jenkins myth. Comic fantasy mythologises Uncle Giles's headquarters, the Ufford, including several metamorphoses. Jenkins fancies that the hotel resembles a ship. It is battleship grey and it looks 'top-heavy', as though 'moored in the street' or 'riding at anchor, on the sluggish Bayswater tides' – in the first chapter of *The Acceptance World*. Its interior, spacious but 'infinitely faded', suggests a Conradian schooner. Uncle Giles dies, in *The Kindly Ones*, at the Bellevue, a seaside hotel run by Albert, formerly the cook at Stonehurst. When he arrives to arrange the funeral, Jenkins discovers that the Bellevue is the Ufford, shrunk and renamed, but recognisably grey and angular: it must have slipped anchor and drifted here. Although obviously unseaworthy, it seems intent on setting out to sea. Uncle Giles is presumably to blame for having imposed his reckless nature on his hotel, 'one of those triumphs of mind over matter' (3).

The Acceptance World also conceives the Ufford to be 'an abode of the dead'. Its public rooms are always deserted and its entry-hall unattended. The passages are catacombs, an underworld for the shabby-genteel (1). Looked at from Uncle Giles's point of view, however, it is a home: 'the old pub suits me'. The narrator concedes in *The Kindly Ones* that Uncle Giles has died 'in one of his own palaces, amongst his own people, the proud, anonymous race that dwell in residential hotels' (3). This genus includes the 'mage', Dr Trelawney, and Myra Erdleigh, the fortune-teller and mistress of the occult. The first meeting with Mrs Erdleigh is at the Ufford, in *The Acceptance World*, where Uncle Giles persuades her to 'put out the cards' to tell his fortune and Nick's. She is completely at home with the other-worldly aspects of the hotel's ambience: she glides over the carpet 'like a phantom' (1). She reappears at the Bellevue, as though to confirm Jenkins's opinion that the Ufford has been removed and transformed, perhaps by her spells, and there too is Dr Trelawney, locked in the bathroom and prophesying war. Uncle Giles pretended to have forgotten Mrs Erdleigh's existence at one stage of the earlier volume, but now she attends his funeral and inherits his money. Duport, also at the seaside hotel, has too much to tell about his own affairs, but he is not a natural Ufford/Bellevue resident. Whatever relations have been between Mrs Erdleigh and Uncle Giles, they will remain secret.

The magic of youth has also touched the Ufford. Young Jenkins is surprised, when the cards are put out, that a man of his uncle's age can be so interested in his future; while 'so far as I myself was concerned, on the other hand, there seemed no reason to curb the wildest absurdity of fancy as to what might happen at the very next moment'. The hotel remains in memory, therefore, as a place of youth and hope, and its transformation by war, in *The Military Philosophers*, comes as a shock. The power that a novel sequence derives from recurring settings as well as from characters and motifs can be observed in the contrast between this episode and Jenkins's stay, in *Temporary Kings*, at the Venetian hotel where he had holidayed with his parents when a boy. Looking back, he muses on 'that eternal question of what constitutes experience' (1). Having heard nothing about the earlier holiday in previous volumes, the reader is less interested in Jenkins's feelings about it than in new details about 'my father'. When Jenkins goes to liaise with the Poles at their headquarters, we guess where he is going before he does; Bayswater is enough to recall the 'sluggish tides' on which the Ufford rode. The double drawing-room with dividing doors leaves no doubt, and we recall how the doors were always closed, and how a reference was made in *The Acceptance World* to the present occasion, suggesting that the doors might be closed only in time of peace, like those of the Roman temple of Janus, double-faced god of gateways. Now, the doors wide open, identification is certain: 'it struck me that the Ufford was in reality the Temple of Janus' (3). Everything has changed at the common novelistic level of appearances: typists and messengers fill the once deserted rooms; a Polish poster has replaced the reproduction of *Bolton Abbey in the Olden Time*, in which Landseer's portrayal of 'medieval plenty' made such a sad contrast to the Ufford's fare. Because we remember the room where Mrs Erdleigh put out the cards, we share the moment when the symbol of Janus springs to mind, and experience 'personal myth' at its most telling.

If Thrubworth Park is a palace or a temple, it is one of Discomfort. Its owner Erridge is the uneasiest of personalities, shifting in his chair 'like a galley-slave during an interval of rest' – in the scene where Thrubworth is introduced, in *At Lady Molly's* (3). His inner discomfort afflicts the one room of the great house in which he now lives. Wondering whether he sleeps here too, Jenkins decides that the sofa looks 'too comfortable to assuage at night-time his guilt for being rich'. Even his social adroitness cannot prevent acute social discomfort in Erridge's presence. Thrubworth yields under the impact of Susan and Isobel, who burst in bringing the news of Susan's engagement, and changing the atmosphere 'violently' with the 'delicious, sparkling proximity of young feminine beings'. Quiggin's proposal of champagne meets fierce resistance, from Erridge and from his alcoholic and malevolent butler Smith. The cellars turn out to contain one last bottle, a Mumm '06, which Erridge would prefer to keep for another occasion. 'Traces of its former excellence', Jenkins's notes, remain in the wine, and the company drink it, in defiance, it seems, of all that Thrubworth represents, although perhaps preserving a tradition from former times.

'True Thrubworth weather', says Norah Tolland as the rain pours down, mist wiping out the landscape, on the day of Erridge's funeral in *Books Do Furnish a Room* (2). The house symbolises melancholy aspects of aristocratic life in a somewhat Dickensian manner: it rains in the hearts of those who feel at home there. Pamela is foremost among them. During the funeral service, Jenkins broods on death, and on Burton's 'vile rock of melancholy', and Pamela seems to have both within her. She disrupts the service, and afterwards vomits into a large Chinese urn, leaving the job of cleaning it out, fraught with inconvenience, to her relations. Siegfried, a wilful German prisoner-of-war who has succeeded Smith, enjoys jostling and interrupting the mourners and forming them into queues for tea. The house has always attracted awkward and uneasy people: Quiggin and Mona were followed, among Erridge's adherents, by St John Clarke (who left his money to Erridge, rescuing Thrubworth's woods from the axe). The funeral brings Widmerpool, Craggs and Gypsy Jones as well as Quiggin. The Jenkinses have opted to stay at the Thrubworth Arms, and readers with something of a Jenkins memory for detail will recall the first words which Lady Isobel speaks in the sequence, on the subject of this hotel.

While Thrubworth is a region of desolation, Stourwater is rich artistically and in literary associations, and is also a source of amusement. Books mentioned in connection with Thrubworth are all unreadable (except in childhood); studies of the Soviet Union, Erridge's bound volumes of boys' comics, St John Clarke's *Fields of Aramanth* in a copy without the binding in the schoolroom cupboard. Literary thoughts in the Thrubworth episodes are gloomy: Burtonian, or otherwise grimly Jacobean. Stourwater is entertaining in its mixture of romantic and worldly associations. It evokes Tennyson, on first encounter, Sir Gavin chanting 'The knights came riding two and two' in *A Buyer's Market (3)*. Late medieval, and 'too perfect' in Sir Gavin's view, it seems to belong to the nineteenth century, or to a nineteenth-century fairyland. Jenkins begins by citing Tennyson and Scott; he feels that a spell might cause it to disappear leaving Sir Magnus 'shivering in rags'. Returning in 1938 (in *The Kindly Ones*), he is disappointed because his memory has rebuilt the place as a magician's castle 'brought into being by some loftier Dr Trelawney'; now it seems only vulgar; even the black swans, which ought to be the work of sorcerers, come from Australia. Moreland, on this occasion, names the castle *'Eldorado banal de tous les vieux garçons'* after Baudelaire's Cythera, island of love. Asked if he thinks love flourishes there, he says love means 'such different things'. Donners has answered him by the end of *The Kindly Ones*, because he has recaptured Matilda, but only, perhaps, by the modern, mundane magic of his money. Moreland is amused by the idea of a castle which is still a powerhouse in the twentieth century; he and Jenkins laugh at its young knights of the metal markets. When it is taken over for government use in 1939, he says he cannot remember why: 'Just as a castle, I suppose.' Its dungeons are a joke to everyone except Widmerpool, because of the part they play in Sir Magnus's fantasies about 'captive maidens' – these, too, have nineteenth-century rather than medieval associations. Jenkins fancies in *A Buyer's Market* that Widmerpool is confined in the dungeons for some offence against the Donners–Brebner conglomerate. The last twist in the castle's fate comes in the final volume when any lingering remnants of Victorian medievalism are dispelled by the schoolgirls' hockey fields.

The War Office and other military headquarters in London tend to be conceived in Wagnerian images. Dull sessions of duty, in *The Military Philosophers*, are transposed into scenes from *The Ring*. A squat lieutenant is Mime at his forge. The War Office's basement, reached by way of 'caves and potholes', is 'an underground kingdom'. High-level staff actually work at these low levels, but 'it might have been thought that Mime and his fellow Nibelungen haunted these murky, subterranean regions'. Movement Control sends, from these depths, armies through land, sea and air, bringing to mind the occult powers of Dr Trelawney, because 'the atmosphere below seemed to demand such highly-coloured metaphor' (1). That sort of metaphor always comes readily to Jenkins. The War Office is linked, within his mythology, with other buildings which at various times in the course of the sequence are shrunk, expanded, removed through the air, metamorphosed, caused to vanish or spring into existence (Shepherd Market, in *A Buyer's Market* (2), thought of as 'another Stonehenge', is subject to 'sorcery' of this kind, for example), repeopled with trolls, goblins or other supernatural figures of legend, by the magic of the mind.

All the various abodes of *Dance* are connected in this way, in a personal geography which is always unpredictable and scarcely to be mapped in all its byways. Some links are obvious. All pubs, including Trapnel's Hero of Acre, recall their archetype the Mortimer, and its *habitué* Mr Deacon, usually because his term for them, 'gin palaces', comes to mind. Mr Deacon is also to be remembered on visits to night-clubs, because he died after falling down the steps of the Bronze Monkey. Peter Templer, who frequents smarter night-clubs, connects them with the Ritz, his natural setting, and so does Dicky Umfraville, hardly to be imagined before *The Valley of Bones* except in night-clubs or the club at Foppa's, because of his promise to tear the Ritz (or Claridge's), apart on the evening of the Le Bas dinner, should he ever attend. Le Bas's house is linked to Sillery's sitting-room, 'burning fiery furnace of adolescent experience', and the shabby sitting-room is linked with the Duports' garishly Italianate interiors of the house in Hill Street where Sillery is present at Milly Andriadis's party. Other connections arise from chance thoughts but are no less strong for that: once established and remembered on later occasions these can be the firmest kind. Stourwater can evoke Stonehurst because the castle is so 'unhaunted', and so lacking, in spite of its age, in the sense of the 'real' past in which the bungalow of childhood is steeped. Stonehurst is linked with the Bellevue because of Albert, but also with the Hay Loft, off the Tottenham Court Road, which served bacon and eggs all night in the later 1920s, frequented with Moreland in those days. This link, at the beginning of the second chapter of *The Kindly Ones*, arises because Jenkins and Moreland have common antecedents in childhood tastes and animosities, and also because 'it is odd to think' of the 'appalling' quantity of experience that had to be lived through before they could meet. Other associations are even more surprising. The Bragadin Palace is linked with the chapel called Sardis, where Jenkins reported for duty in *The Valley of Bones* (1), because the palace in the 'Tiepolo' was at the Lydian capital of Sardis.

The narrator is always attentive to costume, as a means of comparing and classifying people into social psychological types, and as a test. Many poor turn-outs reveal their wearers in predictable ways. Bithel presents himself for wartime duty with egg-stains on his tunic, his trousers soaked in gin-and-italian. Sillery's evening-dress trousers, at Milly Andriadis's party, sag like Charlie Chaplin's. Jenkins is 'snobbishly glad' when London weather is too wet for Mr Deacon's sandals. Quiggins's clothes are deliberately offensive, Jenkins thinks, as part of his left-wing campaign, so long as this lasts. In the 1930s he is expert in the use of black-leather coats, grey shirts and red mufflers; he adopts paramilitary outfits in 1945, after his non-combatant war-years. Gypsy Jones reveals her 'destructive state of mind' in the dirty male-overcoat she wears when seen ranting in the streets in Chapter 4 of *The Kindly Ones*. She is founder of the 'tradition' to which the Quiggin twins adhere when they attend the Magnus Donners Prize Dinner in dirty jeans. Jenkins admires the 'quietly but insistently smart' outfits that help Emily Brightman dissociate herself from 'academic smugness'. He respects Matilda's 'relentless discipline' in preserving her figure and in wearing 'stagey' clothes with style.

He likes those who face the world with 'style', which seems to combine discipline with some other natural flair, lacking in all the ill-clad characters, perhaps an inner harmony destroyed by overactive will. The most stylish people, such as Stringham and Dicky Umfraville, can look distinguished even in old or casual clothes worn on the wrong occasions. Stringham's ancient suit and sweater make Buster look overdressed at Mrs Foxe's party. However lamentably dishevelled, Moreland only looks his stylish self. Trapnel's fancy-dress of military greatcoat, tropical suit, dark glasses and sword-stick are 'brought off' successfully by his rock-like faith in his own 'myth', in spite of Jenkins's alarm at first setting eyes on so disorganised a 'personal superstructure'.

The narrator can, to some extent, persuade readers who do not share his standards (or feel, perhaps, that they would not care to come under Jenkins's sartorial scrutiny), when costumes are comic, and when they are drawn into the mythology of *Dance*. The fact that Peter Templer always looks slightly overdressed, his suits too new, his links too conspicuous, is appropriate and funny because the narrator remembers Stringham's verdict at school that Templer looks as though he is 'going to dance up and down a row of naked ladies'. Buster is too grand to make that mistake, but the way in which – as Stringham says – his clothes are too perfect, overwhelmingly so and therefore not 'elegant', is comically defined at Mrs Foxe's party, where Chandler and Stringham independently grasp the truth about Buster: he goes about as though he were royal, a candidate perhaps to succeed Edward VIII; Stringham wishes he would 'abdicate'. There is humour in Jenkins's reflections and also in his bafflement at the way that 'beauties' can wear anything to good effect, style appearing in their power to adjust their bodies, as much as their clothes, to the demands of fashion or of social and sexual strategy. The former artists' model Mona reveals 'the extraordinary adaptability of women' in the scene at the Ritz in Chapter 2 of *The Acceptance World*. She used to have a sculptor's body which seemed to 'demand instant expression in stone or bronze'. Now, married to Templer, she has altered its lines into a more modest and fashionable 'mould'. When she reappears in *At Lady Molly's*, living with Quiggin, she is, although more 'sluttish' in dress, statuesque once more, a 'strapping' although 'vulgar' Venus in the manner of later classical sculpture (3). Pamela Widmerpool, equally adept, can use any outfit, however smart or sluttish, to discharge her waves of awe and terror.

We are more likely to accept Jenkins's strictures on Widmerpool's attire when he makes them amusing. The famous overcoat at school was wrong because it was worn without any of the 'air' which enables unconventional garments to be worn effectively. Widmerpool gains in confidence, Jenkins notes at the Le Bas dinner, and, a little, in 'air' of dress, but his clothes never fit or look remotely smart, implying a sort of inner or spiritual inelegance. When Jenkins raises a disapproving eyebrow at Widmerpool's bulging form in military uniform, some readers may experience a sneaking sympathy unintended by the author. There are moments, however, when laughter serves the narrator's purpose, as when, in *Hearing Secret Harmonies*, the television camera observes Widmerpool processing as Chancellor of a new university and pausing in altercation with the page who is carrying the train of his robes. That is a particularly good sight-line. Widmerpool there is what Powell always wants him to be, indignity incarnate.

Costume is most effectively used when linked with other elements in the narrator's private imaginative world. The notion of 1939–45 as 'a tailor's war' sometimes seems contrived: in the first pages of *A Soldier's Art*, for example, the haberdasher who sells Jenkins an army greatcoat in 1939 is, Jenkins fancies, so completely absorbed in the theatrical side of his business that he has failed to notice the outbreak of war, wishing his customer success in his new show. It is predictable that while Pennistone is able to carry off the 'incisive demands of uniform', Widmerpool as a Territorial in *The Kindly Ones*, looks like Heather Hopkins as a stage admiral about to sing a comic song. Lieutenant Cheesman, however, who succeeds Bithel in command of the mobile laundry, is funny and impressive in his refusal to stop wearing the waistcoat of civilian life (as an accountant): he has one cut from the tunic material. It is by this waistcoat that Jenkins remembers him when he thinks of Stringham imprisoned with the laundry after the fall of Singapore, in the last chapter of *The Military Philosophers*. There it has become, in the narrator's terms, a 'significant' garment, an essential feature of the laundry's own myth. The red breeches worn by Clanwaert when he fought his first battle become mythical because of the name the Belgian attaché insists on for their colour: 'Not *red*, my friend – this is important – *amaranthe*. How do you say that in English?' Clanwaert's stress on the explicit term would in itself be enough to win Jenkins's respect. 'Amaranth' does more. It forges a link between the whole imaginative world of military uniforms, extending away to those worn at Stonehurst by 'my father', and, in even more remote times, by General Conyers, and the other world, equally rich in myth, of St John Clarke and his writings. In the roll-call of his novels, *Match Me Such Marvel, The Heart is Highland, E'en the Longest River, Never to the Philistines, Mimosa* and *Dust Thou Art, Fields of Amaranth* has pride of place, a book that, however much it is to be deplored in later life, everyone of Jenkins's generation has enjoyed when young. He immediately tells Clanwaert about the novel, and we learn of its play on the two strands in the flower's legend: its being 'unfading' and its English name, 'love lies bleeding'. Clanwaert says that the name is 'too good for a pair of breeches', but Jenkins disagrees. Henceforth St John Clarke is linked in his mind with the attachés of *The Military Philosophers* (2). The comedy lies in Jenkins's inevitable delight in this *trouvaille*, redeeming a day of dull duty, making a surprising bond between two disparate characters and spheres of his life, and connecting one 'seam of Time' (his phrase) with another.

War and peace are both 'shows' in the sense that the narrator recostumes his cast in his imagination. The look of King Lear achieved by the unkempt figure of Craggs the publisher at Erridge's funeral must owe something to former association with Mr Deacon, Jenkins thinks, because he and Gypsy resembled Lear and the Fool in the storm, on the night when they were met selling *War Never Pays!*. The street where he has his shop looks like the background for a harlequinade, so that 'I was almost prepared for Mr Deacon, with mask and spangles and magic wand, suddenly to pirouette along the pavement'. Mr Deacon is extremely adaptable in fancy. If not Lear, he might be Peter the Hermit. His sandals and black socks confirm 'his medieval air' (*A Buyer's Market*, 2, 3, 2). His incarnations go further back in time. He appears in one of his own pictures at the Henderson exhibition as a Roman citizen in a toga (rebuking a slave-boy). The distant past of his Mortimer days, Jenkins thinks, and Roman times are equally remote to young Henderson. Sir Gavin's formidable sister, Miss Walpole-Wilson, who belongs to the same, *A Buyer's Market* era, dresses in browns and greens, with hats that appear to be peaked, so that she seems to belong 'to some dedicated order of female officials, connected possibly with public service in the woods and forests, with responsibilities 'difficult for a lay person – even impossible if a male . . . to understand' (3). The acting of the Sins is a central scene in *Dance* because so many of its characters, including these two, are only an imaginative step away from performing in charades. The narrator collects examples of how the characters imagine one another. Chandler pictures Carolo, at the *Seraglio*, in the black velvet suit and lace collar in which he played when a child-prodigy. Moreland thinks Chandler, on the same occasion, a Teddy Boy (*Temporary Kings*, 5). Stringham discovers by a stroke of intuitive genius that Mrs Maclintick's pink dress covered in rosettes, bows and frills, worn at his mother's party in *Casanova's Chinese Restaurant*, is that of Little Bo-Peep, putting an immediate stop to the rage she is in against Maclintick. The hockey-field at Stourwater prompts Gwinnett to talk about Aztec sport and Fiona to picture the present-day scene if the Aztec custom were to be followed: on the scoring of a goal, the spectators' clothes and jewels 'were forfeit to the players' (*Hearing Secret Harmonies*, 6).

A phrase in Chapter 2 of this last volume shows how various mythical strands can be drawn together from many parts of the sequence. Remembering Dr Trelawney, brought to mind by Scorpio Murtlock, the narrator says that while his disciples' tunics used to be of pastel shades, 'the Doctor's robe (like the undefiled of Sardis) was white'. That is in the Stonehurst days when the child Nicholas has frightening daydreams of belonging to the disciples. The allusion to Sardis recalls the text from Revelation (3:4) inscribed in huge gothic letters on the wall of the chapel in *The Valley of Bones*: 'Thou hast a few names even in Sardis which have not defiled their garments: and they shall walk with me in white: for they are worthy' (1). We must now think of Jacky Bragadin's palace as well as of the regiment in Wales. Scorpio Murtlock seems even more bizarre in connection with those who may walk in white than Dr Trelawney, since, walking across the field at Stourwater he resembles Apollyon 'come to contend' in *Pilgrim's Progress*, an image of the King of Hell which 'riveted' Jenkins and Moreland in their childhoods. Murtlock and his male followers wear blue robes, a cause of mild social embarrassment to Jenkins when he and they meet the dignified farmer Mr Gauntlet and he refers to the crayfishing as though the robes were usual for that sport. It is Widmerpool, not Jenkins, who has to join the oddly clad disciples not of Trelawney but of Murtlock, who claims to be the Doctor's successor. The idea of undefiled garments suggests Jenkins's views about good turn-out: Bithel's egg-stains and Gypsy's grubbiness are properly condemned, he would consider, by 'the Apocalyptic verdict of the walls'. Widmerpool has always mismanaged his garment; recently, he has defiled it. The scarlet sweater worn for the Magnus Donners Prize Dinner is torn and dirty by the time of the Royal Academy banquet. He has, moreover, provoked others into defiling him – long ago when Barbara Goring poured the sugar, and lately in the procession as Chancellor, when covered with red paint by the Quiggin twins, treatment he has welcomed on principle. It could be argued that he deserves to be reduced first to the blue robe and finally to nakedness. That is certainly an appropriate fate within the scheme of things in *Dance*. Nakedness has been an intermittent motif in the sequence, sometimes merely erotic, sometimes comic, as in the scene, central in the myths of Jenkins's childhood, where the maid Billson gives notice in the drawing-room as naked as the Queen of Sardis. Widmerpool's last naked run is a gruesome ending but one which extends back comically throughout this fictional world.

There are many other recurrent motifs, but a surprising number of them are linked with pictures, places or costume. The Eumenides, to be classed with Janus and Candaules among those from classical myth or legend, belong, with its ghost, to Stonehurst where Albert tried in vain to put up the shutters against them in the stable-block in the late afternoon. The Furies first stripped Billson of her 'raiment', showing their absolute power over those in love, and then unleashed the Great War. Casanova, a favourite of Jenkins's among figures of modern legend, is inseparable from his Chinese Restaurant, where the pastel frescoes 'appealed to Heaven knows what nadir of aesthetic degradation' (1). The practical jokes and eccentric acts of Lord Vowchurch, father of Bertha Conyers and Mildred Haycock, make stories often retold: he put a clockwork mouse into the sleeve of his overcoat when Albert, then with the Alfords, was helping him into it at the door – 'one of the great adventures of Albert's life'; in another he rode his favourite hunter upstairs after dinner, a whole side of the house, at Melton-Mowbray, afterwards having to be removed to free the horse. Copies of St John Clarke's books are potent things, in narrative terms; the finding of one, or mention of one's whereabouts, will result in a pause, stirring memories. *Dust Thou Art* appears in Jenkins's room in college when he returns to the university to work on Burton; *Never to the Philistines* is one of four books in the smoking-room at Stonehurst; in this way places in different 'seams of Time' are joined. Whatever is most enjoyable to remember turns into myth as it is told, and so builds up the narrative, endlessly interrelated and always generating new relations, like memory itself.

5

A Dance to the Music of Time: Voices

Powell's best characters come to life in their talk. The pairings and groups in which they converse and comment on one another are often surprising. Any voice can break in at any point in the story, regardless of time and place. Not only do the characters 'on stage' constantly interrupt the narrator; other members of his cast intervene to comment, even when they belong to different eras of his life, past or future. This is noticeable in the first chapter of *The Kindly Ones*.

The last two weeks of normal Stonehurst life, before war ended it, are reconstructed there from memories of the saga of Billson, related so often afterwards by 'my mother'. Life is most 'intense' and interesting, for the child Nicholas, in the kitchen where the maid Billson, hopelessly loved by the soldier–servant Bracey, hopelessly loves Albert. Powell is limited in what he can do with the voices of servants and soldiers. Some of the Welsh troops in the war volumes are fully convincing only as 'what the narrator heard', as Powell admits.[50] The Sergeant-Major in the first pages of *The Valley of Bones* is among the best: '"Some of the new intake was taught different to fold them blankets," said the Sergeant-Major cautiously.' Grammatical dialect-features and a lilt that sounds authentic also produce the talk of the Stonehurst kitchen, enriched by the sort of unintentionally memorable phrases that stick in the minds of children. 'I should not wish to cross the Captain in any of his appetites', Albert says, discussing a savoury for dinner. It is Albert who renames the Furies (or Suffragettes):

> 'Don't want any of them Virgin Marys busting in and burning the place down.'
>
> 'Can't tell what those hussies will do next.'

Escaping from his nurse Edith on the days when she is incapacitated by 'small aches and pains few people die of', Nicholas hears confusingly unorthodox accounts of the army. '"Anyway," said Billson, "I wouldn't have a soldier ... Tommies are all the same."' Bracey suffers 'funny days' when overwhelmed by regulations.

'Shall I help you to a plate then, Private Bracey?'
'If it's my right, I'll have a plate.'
'Then I'll give you some stew?'
'If it's my right.'

On normal days he expresses frankly a Private's view of soldiering: 'Them Redcaps aren't loved all that.' The Military Police are too fond of getting a bloke 'a spell of clink'.

'Some blokes want to get even when they comes out.'
'How?'
'Waits behind a hedge on a dark night.'

Powell achieves more individuality of tone in the speech of 'my parents', merging belief in the ghosts with an Edwardian sense of domestic duty in 'my mother': 'it really is not fair on servants to expect them to sleep in a haunted room, although I have to myself'; and giving 'my father' just the right mix of jesting and attack when he meets his brother: 'How has the world been wagging with you, Giles?'

Other voices intrude into Stonehurst from far away. The voice of Sunny Farebrother is heard, contradicting the cynicism of Bracey's opinion that 'Rifle and bayonet's a man's best friend when he goes to battle', and confirming the ethos of Nicholas's adventure stories. Sunny is remembered from Jenkins's War Office period, speaking of his love of Henty's *For Name and Fame; or, Through Khyber Pass*, for its truth to the joy of 'comradeship under arms'. When Dr Trelawney frightens 'my mother' in the Post Office, intoning his ritual greeting, wearing his robe, appearing to bless the post-mistress, the masterful tones of Mr Deacon break through the seams of time to talk at length on a subject with which he is at home:

Too much abracadabra about Trelawney. ... Human beings

> are sad dupes I fear. . . . 'The Vision of Visions heals the Blindness of Sight,' forsooth. I was too free a spirit for Trelawney in spite of his denial of the World. Still, some of his early views on diet were on the right track.

Utter conviction rings in Mr Deacon's words and cadences. 'Abracadabra', is the only word for Trelawney, forsooth. The sense of one expert in the non-conformism of the time appraising another, and, the last words stress, aiming to be fair, gives the Doctor a social solidity Scorpio Murtlock never achieves. Murtlock is also at a disadvantage in that Trelawney is so well embedded in time. Mr Deacon's verdict reaches forward and back: his words belong to the period covered five volumes earlier, although fifteen years after Stonehurst, and more than twenty years before the time of narration.

David Pennistone makes an authoritative comment, from the time of *The Military Philosophers*, relevant to assessing 'my father': 'these senior officers are a lot of ballerinas', and the narrator adds that General Conyers's praise of luncheon was not entirely pleasing to his host because 'my father . . . grew easily tired of hearing another man, even his own cook, too protractedly commended'. Uncle Giles is due to arrive later on Billson's funny afternoon, but his voice intrudes into the Billson incident, from a different occasion, making a good example of how a speaker from *Dance*'s background chorus can comment on a scene from outside, as though captioning a picture. The clock-time of the maid's appearance, announcement of 'notice' and removal by Conyers can be hardly more than a minute. The incident occupies six pages of this chapter. While the general is escorting Billson to her room (in the action we are to imagine), four paragraphs are devoted to thoughts about his success. One line of reflection leads to his reputation, before marriage, as a man with 'a natural aptitude for handling "women"'.

> 'Aylmer Conyers couldn't keep away from the women as a young man,' Uncle Giles once remarked. 'They say some fellow chaffed him about it at a big viceregal bun-fight at Delhi – Henry Wilson or another of those talkative beggars who later became generals – "Aylmer, my boy," this fellow, whoever he was, said, "you're digging your grave in bed with Mrs Roxborough-Brown and the rest of them," he said. Conyers didn't give a dam. Not a dam. Went on just the same.'

These remnants of the General's 'prehistoric' past combine with the image of his 'handling' of Billson, enriching the comedy, driving new fissures through the seams of time, and, in a way typical of the narrative method of the sequence, giving a character extraneous to the cast of the particular scene a distinctive voice ('chaffed', 'beggars', 'bun-fight') in its narration.

Powell's achievement in dialogue can be called 'Dickensian'. Any English novelist who creates character through speech habits has to be measured by that standard. One Dickensian feature of *Dance* is the exuberance of figures of fun, such as Myra Erdleigh, Mark Members and Uncle Giles, who have such marked styles that the narrator cannot resist them. Mr Deacon is one of the best. He is also a good example of the fact that, whether or not there is, as Mrs Erdleigh and Dr Trelawney maintain, no death in nature, there is none in fiction. Three volumes after his death in *A Buyer's Market*, he sits in the Mortimer (about a week before his death), in the first chapter of *Casanova's Chinese Restaurant*, and talks:

> As I was remarking Nicholas, I have come to this gin-palace primarily to inspect an object of virtu – a classical group in some unspecified material, to be precise. I shall buy it, if its beauty satisfies me. *Truth Unveiled by Time* – in the Villa Borghese, you remember. I must say in the original marble Bernini has made the wench look as unpalatable as the heartless quality she represents. A reproduction of this work was found at the Caledonian Market by a young person with whom I possess a slight acquaintance.

The homosexual overtones, beyond Dickens's range, in 'young person', a phrase jumped on at once by Moreland, and in the characteristic disdain for 'the female form divine' (Dicky Umfraville's term borrowed elsewhere to point out the absence of women from Deacon's pictures), combine well with the art-school instructor's pedantic note and with a parsonic cadence and old-maidish prissiness. An actor would be attracted by the chance to sound out the words 'gin-palace' and 'wench' in the setting of this speech.

Sillery's synthetic talk, full of dialect, Americanisms and stale literary phraseology (and, some say, fossil traces of Sir Maurice Bowra), guys donnish affectation of the sort that veils intent of purpose. It also suits the character's boundless egotism. He is rightly pictured as a monkey, bounding about his college room, because his will has an animal's natural energy. He tells Jenkins and Short about his peerage, in the first chapter of *Books Do Furnish a Room*.

> 'Ain't it absurd?' he shouted. 'As you'll have guessed, my dear Nick, I didn't want the dratted thing at all. . . . A Peer of the Realm. Who'd have prophesied that for crude young Sillers, that happy-go-lucky little fellow, in the days of yore? It certainly gave some people here furiously to think.'

He is so successful a caricature that he is to be recognised in places far from his college: '"You can't close your ears to gossip in this university, however much you try," said Sillery.' He has the Chaucerian or Theophrastian strength of representing a type which will last, in his case at least as long as Oxford; inseparable perhaps from academic institutions, however constituted. In Quiggin the satire is more narrow and feels more forced, although it records and mocks the jargon, known from so many other sources, of parlour-socialism in the 1930s: 'The Lewis gun may be sounding at the barricades earlier than some of your Laodicean friends think.' Culture in arms is implied by combining the obscure reference to agnostics (Revelation 3: 14–18) with precise knowledge of modern weaponry, as though in a 1930s poem influenced by Stephen Spender.

Quiggin combines this patter with Northernisms (dialect uncertain), wielded when required for social advantage. This is what Sillery calls his 'Doric' voice, Jenkins his 'harsh geniality', to be heard in the same chapter of *At Lady Molly's*: 'But you know, Alf, you really ought to celebrate rightly in a bottle of champagne' (3). Some characters, including Erridge and the smoothly avant-garde Members, make him good foils. He only talks well, however, in his own element. He is a pale figure at Templer's house in *The Acceptance World*, and reduced to a mere publisher in the last three volumes. The old Quiggin would never have let himself be out-talked as he is by Ada (now Mrs Quiggin) when she subdues him over the St John Clarke broadcast in *Hearing Secret Harmonies*:

> 'The television of the body brings the sales everlasting.'

Quiggin bowed his head.
'Amen . . .' (2)

Powell makes little use of Quiggin in the last volumes, as though acknowledging that without his Marxism he is a spent force conversationally. Bagshaw takes over some of his roles. Mark Members, however, in discourse ever more glibly witty and allusive, develops into a prince of letters in the television age.

Canon Fenneau is an example of how effectively a manner of speaking can be described. Fenneau shares Mrs Erdleigh's occult phraseology; he is, the narrator decides, akin to her in essentials, 'in spite of what was, no doubt, a minor matter, difference of sex'. These elements possess a more academic tone in him, and coexist easily with a mandarin prose proper for an Anglican cleric of high caste: his passion for alchemy, he says, 'has always gripped me – naturally in a manner not to run counter to my cloth'. The motions of his lips and expressions of his eyes contribute to the effect of his words: his mouth, which he can extend 'into ogreish proportions', tightens, the mistiness of his eyes hardening, when he mentions his bishop, so that the narrator imagines the bishop turned into a toad or locked in a hollow oak. The formidable strength of his will can be heard in the determined inflections of the voice, at the end of his one scene in the last volume, as he makes absolutely certain that Jenkins will send books for his Christmas bazaar. The idea that Widmerpool has met his match is appropriately conveyed:

> 'Canon Fenneau, I think?'
> 'Your servant.'
> Cannon Fenneau said that like a djinn rising vaporously from an unsealed bottle. (4)

Characters of this rich individuality do not necessarily consort easily, although Jenkins always hopes to get them to talk about one another, and if possible to meet. Le Bas and Mr Deacon decline to comment on Sillery (whom, of course, they both know). Sillery merely warns Jenkins against being seen talking too long with Mr Deacon. It is hard to imagine a meeting of Mr Deacon and Uncle Giles. Mr Deacon's comments on Quiggin, in *A Buyer's Market* (4), are funny, but brief. The Dance, which seems to require that some characters belong together (Members and

Quiggin, Mr Deacon and Gypsy Jones), also follows aesthetic judgment on what will mix in keeping others apart.

Powell might be compared with Dickens in his power to vary styles within one species of talker, red-faced men or lawyers in Dickens, literary people, hostesses and generals (among other groups) in Powell. The party to launch *Fission*, magazine for the atomic age, in *Books Do Furnish a Room*, assembles literary talkers. Bernard Shernmaker, a reviewer so high-brow that he is almost incapable of praise, out-Quiggins Quiggin as 'a punch-line killer'. Asked not to 'wash his hands' of Alaric Kydd, one of Quiggin's novelists, he answers after due pause, 'Pilate washed his hands – did he wash his feet?' (3). While Shernmaker speaks only in such discouraging aphorisms, Members's talk flows freely, pouring forth a lament about travel restrictions, fatal to artists, under Attlee's regime. The novelist Evadne Clapham brightly quotes Blake's 'Robin Redbreast in a Cage' and Shernmaker smashes this, reversing 'Cage and Rage' to improve the couplet – but in vain, because she brightly assumes that he is supporting her. Bagshaw talks on about Marx and Feuerbach even when drunk and dancing with Evadne. Socialism is a pure intellectual passion in Bagshaw, whose disillusionment with the cause does not stop him talking. Odo Stevens speaks in very practical terms about the advantages of a publisher keen on 'Commies'. Bagshaw can be practical too, as editor of *Fission*, about the thinkers of the far left; his remark of this era is recalled in *Temporary Kings*: 'If we've got to print everything written by whoever's rogering Gypsy, we'll have to get a new paper allowance' (3). Trapnel is an example of an imaginative speaker who, not a drinker, becomes drunk on volubility. He talks such nonsense to Widmerpool that Jenkins thinks he is trying to start a quarrel. Widmerpool takes all that Trapnel and everyone else says literally and leaves the party bemused.

Hostesses and generals are groups of speakers where individual members do not easily mix, although the narrator enjoys comparing and contrasting. Hostesses vary in scale: one goes to tea at the Conyerses'; Milly Andriadis has everyone at her great Hill Street party, from Prince Theodoric to Gypsy Jones. 'You darlings', Milly says, contemplating Stringham's frightful assortment of extra guests, 'it is going to be a lovely party now' (*A Buyer's Market*, 2). The narrator broods about the style the sisters Bertha Conyers and Mildred Haycock share in spite of the fact that there is scarcely a speech of Mildred's, either in her 1914–18 era of almost solid slang or in her 'fast' talk of the 1930s, that Mrs Conyers could have uttered. Mrs Foxe is very fast indeed, and deplores the 'slowness' of Lady Huntercombe, but she is also 'grand' in Templer's (deprecating) use of the term. She disclaims the idea, which she associates with 'Buck House' and royal 'stuffiness' of the sort in which Lady Frederica Tolland, a lady-in-waiting in the 1930s, is at home (until she marries Dicky Umfraville). Her report, at the end of her party, on how she talked to the drunk Maclintick, who was falling down her front-steps, would make good material for a socio-linguist. Her passion for dominating people can be heard in all she says: will-power has helped in making her the most awesome of the hostesses. Lady Molly is the warmest, taking in the homeless Moreland, whom she has never seen before, when she meets him at the vet's, at the end of *The Kindly Ones*. Her household seems pleasantly ramshackle, in contrast to the disciplined headquarters of her sister, Katherine, Lady Warminster, Jenkins's step-mother-in-law, at Hyde Park Gardens. It is also livelier; guests are introduced to the monkey kept in her bedroom, named Maisky after the Soviet ambassador of the day. It is not to be forgotten, however, that she was Marchioness of Sleaford at eighteen, and knows what social power is. The narrator traces in her style 'a noisy, absolutely unrestrained directness of manner ... of a kind that suggested both simplicity of nature and certainty of her own position: both characteristics that can stimulate that streak of social cruelty that few lack' (*At Lady Molly's*, 1). Widmerpool's mother, inevitably, is the nastiest of hostesses.

> 'Shall we leave the gentlemen to their port?' said Mrs Widmerpool. . . .
>
> She mouthed the words 'gentlemen' and 'port' as if they might be facetiously disputable as strictly literal descriptions in either case. (*A Buyer's Market*, 4)

The term 'mouthed' has never been found a better setting.

The narrator likes to compare generals in their intellectual and literary aspects, amused especially by ways in which military crispness, directness and decision conflict with the open, sceptical, even vacillating habits of customary literary discourse. General Liddament speaks of Trollope as though of an army manual on basic training.

'You've never found Trollope easy to read?'
'No, sir.'
He was clearly unable to credit my words. This was an unhappy situation. There was a long pause while he glared at me.
'Why not?' he asked at last.
He spoke very sternly. I tried to think of an answer. (*The Soldier's Art*, 1)

Jenkins's attempt at a critical defence of his position is dismissed in one word: 'Rubbish'. The scene is a good example of 'naturalism' in *Dance*; the temptation, given so very strong a comic situation, to pass beyond what might plausibly be said is avoided. Liddament is not 'caricatured' in the sense that the speeches of Sillery, Quiggin, Mr Deacon are improvements on the actual utterances to be imagined in such persons in life. Naturalism seems to be earned by the author's respect. Powell is amused by the clash of modes of talk, not by General Liddament, who picks out the one point in all Jenkins says that has practical bearing. Leaving aside critical discussion of Balzac, he asks, 'Read him in French?' It is Jenkins who makes a fool of himself then. Although he is not to be imagined raising his voice in literary debate, General Conyers is also direct, exacting a yes-or-no answer, hard to obtain from Jenkins, on whether he liked *Orlando*. While Liddament is an intelligent middle-brow (in Virginia Woolf's terminology), Conyers is high-brow, completely ignoring his wife's attempt to bring St John Clarke's work into the conversation. His years as a courtier have polished him but he has never acquired the trappings of talk among professional intellectuals: abandoning Jungian interpretation of Widmerpool he says 'I'll open another field of fire' (*At Lady Molly's*, 5). The consistently first-class quality of his mind can be noticed in his questioning of Nicholas at Stonehurst.

Parties, from Mayfair to Mortimer, are the sequence's great arenas of talk, and the best encounter, although surprisingly one-sided in the event, is between Stringham (supported by Mrs Maclintick) and Moreland, at Mrs Foxe's party in Chapter 3 of *Casanova's Chinese Restaurant*. These two are closest to Jenkins in appreciation of the talk of other characters. Templer's comment on Widmerpool at school in the first volume, 'he's so wet you could shoot snipe off him', is quoted by Stringham as 'an exquisitely Templer phrase' (1), to be valued as a sort of clubman's equivalent to poetry. Moreland shares Jenkins's amusement at the extraordinary conversational banality of Sir Magnus Donners. Stringham and Moreland are able combatants, Stringham making it appear, in the first volume, that he has ordered Buster from the room; Moreland effortlessly fending off verbal attack by Mark Members ('How is sweet music?'), going in to see *The Duchess of Malfi*, in the first chapter of volume 5. Both talk well in any circumstances, Stringham on the verge of alcoholic collapse, Moreland when exhausted, ill and abandoned by Matilda at the end of *The Kindly Ones*. Stringham is a socially charming wit, skilfully casual with aphorisms; Moreland is given to elaborate flights of fancy, wearying to some characters. Stringham's melancholy is chronic, Moreland's intermittent, frequently overcome or merged in the high spirits that shake him with laughter. They represent the two realms of Jenkins's peace-time life – Stringham high ('smart') society and Moreland the arts.

Stringham's alliance with Mrs Maclintick makes an interesting combination in the Dance since Moreland, at present meditating adultery with Priscilla Tolland, is to live with Mrs Maclintick after Matilda has gone back to Donners. It is also a surprising and successful pairing of two completely different speakers. Mrs Foxe has asked Moreland's friends with the result that a corner of her crimson drawing-room looks like the Mortimer. While Lord Huntercombe prizes open cabinets with his penknife ('What nice china there is in this house'), Mrs Maclintick's characteristic note sounds discordantly: '"Do take your hands out of your pockets Maclintick," she said at once ... "We are not in the Nag's Head now ...".' 'Drunk' is too crude a term for Stringham's condition, the narrator reflects: his particular state at present is one of 'controlled exhilaration'. His natural 'dash', heightened in this way and mixed with memories of his ruined marriage, gives him 'conversational mastery' over Mrs Maclintick, and over Moreland. She is first silenced by the nursery language suited to his idea of her as little Bo-Peep, then charmed by his affected gallantry and incisive strictures on Maclintick's general appearance. Being helpless with laughter puts Moreland at a disadvantage, but he is out-talked chiefly because Stringham's long prose-lament on marriage belongs to a different genre of talk from his own, one marked by a 'bitter grasp of social circumstance'.

Stringham is amused and embittered by the extent to which Mountfichet is an unmusical house – dirges would have cheered up the morning-room; by the colour of the Earl of Bridgnorth's face at breakfast; by the awful judgment on his sister-in-law of marrying Dicky Umfraville, in ways belonging to a different region of the imagination than Moreland's. Symphonies, operas and plays feed Moreland's mind and talk; country houses and family histories Stringham's. This is one of the best dramatic scenes in the sequence and one where Powell fully succeeds in the aim of combining comedy with the grotesque when Stringham is silenced and led away into his alcoholic confinement, subject to the icy will of his keeper, Tuffy Weedon. Summoned by Buster on the orders of Mrs Foxe, she removes 'dear Charles', whose nerves are so bad these days that it is better for him not to stay up late.

Many of Powell's talkers enjoy quotations. These can illustrate character. Sir Gavin is just the man to quote, in *A Buyer's Market* (1), Elroy Flecker's *Hassan*: '"For lust of knowing what we should not know," he was fond of intoning, "we take the Golden Road to Samarkand."' His failure as a diplomatist who was 'unstuck' adds a pleasing dimension to that line. Quotation can give a naturalistic edge to literary talkers. Ada Leintwardine says at the *Fission* party that Evadne Clapham's coiffure reminds her of Arthur Symons's 'And is it seaweed in your hair?' Ideas with potential bearing on Powell's theme arise in talk modified by varying attitudes. David Pennistone, who speaks with intellectual authority, quotes Nietzsche's 'eternal recurrences', perhaps a theory to 'explain' the Dance. Moreland, who speaks for the arts, implies that this philosopher is not to be taken too seriously, 'one touch of Nietzsche makes the whole world kin', in *Books Do Furnish a Room* (3), recalling to Jenkins's mind Pennistone's words in *The Soldier's Art* (3). Moreland quotes profusely from English and French literature, but he does so most effectively when he joins the narrator in finding new images for the poetic realm of the sequence. Baudelaire's *Cythère*, '*Eldorado banal*', improves Stourwater's myth. Moreland thought of as composer among the music critics is Tamburlaine the Great among the captive kings as soon as Matilda mentions Christopher Marlowe's play:

'Holla, ye pampered jades of Asia,' he cried. 'What, can ye

draw but twenty miles a day?' That is rather what I feel about the newspaper criticism of Gossage and Maclintick. I should like them to drag me to concerts as the kings drew Tamerlaine, in a triumphal coach. (*Casanova's Chinese Restaurant*, 1)

Moreland extrapolates further surrealist scenes from this conceit of the slow-trudging reviewers; he is still reanimating literature in his last days, 'researching' the place of the vintage motor-car in the history of English verse.

Quotations are most attractive throughout the sequence when they add to or connect with Jenkins's mythology. Many sorts of songs are remembered. Max Pilgrim's nightclub songs of 'Tess of Le Touquet' and 'Di, Di in her collar and tie' are 'chanted continuously' as though a 'saga recording the heroic, legendary deeds of some primitive race' (*A Buyer's Market*, 2); they are sagas belonging to their own epoch, that of the later 1920s and early 1930s, to be sharply contrasted with the innocent merriment of earlier ages, so that Ted Jeavons, fixed in the period of the Great War, still singing 'If you were the only girl in the world', cannot understand a word of them. The songs and hymns of the Welsh soldiers of the war volumes shrink history rather than enlarging it because they seem timeless: 'Ten bob a week, / Bugger all to eat, / Great big boots and blisters on your feet' – soldiers always sang of such grievances. In *The Military Philosophers*, we hear the last of the men of Jenkins's regiment singing 'Open now the crystal fountain' as they march eastwards from south Holland, not into the Third Reich but 'towards the urnfields of their Bronze Age home' (4).

Stringham shares something of Le Bas's taste for late-nineteenth-century Hellenistic lyric verse. Uncle Giles occasionally takes refuge, during quarrels with the Ufford, at a nearby hotel called the De Tabley, so that when Jenkins approaches the Temple of Janus in *The Military Philosophers*, he remembers how Le Bas and Stringham discussed Lord de Tabley's 'Sweet are the ways of death to weary feet'; the whole scene at school is reconstructed, nine volumes after its chronological place, so that another fissure is driven through the seams of Time. Stringham is also addicted to hymns, quoting to Tuffy 'Not for ever by still waters / Would we idly rest and stay' when surrendering to her authority at his mother's party. Hymns, therefore, always recall Stringham to Jenkins's mind, as they do at the victory service in St Paul's, where he thinks of how Stringham liked the explicitness of the categories, capturing so perfectly 'one's friends and relations' in

> Some are sick and some are sad,
> And some have never loved one well,
> And some have lost the love they had.

Recollection of Stringham at school brings 'thoughts about Singapore', and so revives for a moment Cheesman, commander of the imprisoned laundry, and his military waistcoat.

That is near the end of *The Military Philosophers*, the volume where Jenkins is closest to the great events of his time and the one where he puts them most firmly in the background. There are many able talkers here, including Pennistone, himself a connoisseur of the talk of others, enjoying Finn's 'extraordinary French' ('*Le Commandant-Chef aime bien les garçons*' – of a memo from on high approving the recruitment of young Poles as cadets, 1). Mrs Erdleigh manifests herself during an air-raid, and quotes to Pamela, from Desbarrolles, terrible words of warning. Her talk and that of Dr Trelawney is made up from scraps of occult reading; he hails her, at the Bellevue in *The Kindly Ones*, as '*la vieille souveraine du monde*', and 'priestess of Isis', because she has escaped 'the puny fingers of Time' (3). Such cabalistic dialectic always adds to the comic treatment of the theme of dancing to Time's music. Jenkins constantly quotes to himself, in this volume; hearing gunfire, he reaches for culture. He and his (well-chosen) assistant, Corporal Curtis, do fire-duty on the War Office roof on a night when flying bombs are coming over the Thames. It is hard to imagine another war-novelist who, coming at last to a scene of 'action', would make the officer order the NCO: 'Tell me the plot of *Adam Bede* as far as you've got. I've never read it' (3). It is for such moments, perhaps, that Powell's admirers love him best. When a V1 falls on Lambeth, the same line of Spenser, quoted in *The Waste Land*, occurs to both men:

'Sweet Thames run softly . . .'
'I was thinking the same, sir.'

Curtis knows how a literary corporal should bear himself, and he finishes off the plot of *Adam Bede*.

A comparable disdain for war appears in more lavish quotations. A page and a half of Proust (the Princess of Guermantes's party, translated) illustrates Jenkins's reading during the blitz. The Field-Marshal's talk to put the military attachés 'in the picture', on the visit to his headquarters, is obliterated by a flow of quotation and musing that distracts Jenkins's mind from paying any attention to this insider-account of the state of the war, and most of the victory service is supplanted in the same way. Some quotations are better integrated than others. The Proust prepares for the distinctly Powellian incident of the General and the bathroom at Cabourg, Proust's Balbec. One of the verses Jenkins remembers while he ought to be listening to the Field-Marshal links the Earl of Rochester with Dicky Umfraville, who would have found themes of common interest to discuss with the Restoration poet, because 'Yarmouth leaguer', mentioned in Rochester's verses on a drinking cup, appears to have been the sort of transit camp Umfraville formerly commanded.[51] *The Ingoldsby Legends*, recalled by the monumental sculptures in St Paul's which Barham's book describes – although 'that queer-looking horse that is rolling on Ponsonby' cannot be located among the scenes they depict – take Jenkins back to Stonehurst where the *Legends* were favourite childhood reading.

One of the happiest ventures in this kind of intertextuality is the role of Ariosto's *Orlando Furioso*, in Harington's verse translation of 1591, in *Hearing Secret Harmonies*. The narrator quotes a twelve-line stanza because he thinks its details coincide with Scorpio Murtlock's cray-fishing visit. He comments that one of the solaces of age is 'a keener perception of the authenticities of mythology, not only of the traditional sort, but – when such are any good – the latter-day mythologies of poetry and the novel' (2). One correspondence is between Orlando and Widmerpool, since both 'drop out' of society, become deranged and abandon their clothing. An even better discovery concerns Ariosto's character Astolpho, an English duke who travels to the moon, riding on a hippogryph, and finds in the lunar Valley of Lost Things, Orlando's wits, among a lot more of this world's lost property.[52] When St John Clarke is restored to fame by the television broadcast, it is obvious that Mrs Quiggin has salvaged his reputation from the Valley on the moon. Ariosto was 'keen on transvestism', his poem including many 'maidens clad in armour', so that Ada is 'a perfectly concordant Ariosto character'. Later in the novel,

Barnabas Henderson replaces her, taking on Astolpho's role in order to rescue Mr Deacon's paintings from the Valley of Lost Things.

The narrator's voice asserts itself from first to last. It is most characteristic when most leisurely and mannered, in the epic similes, for example. Jenkins meets Ted Jeavons for the first time in *At Lady Molly's*:

> Like one of those mammoths – or, in Jeavons's case, somewhat less gigantic form of primeval life – caught in a glacier and physically preserved into an age when his very kind was known only from fossilised bones, or drawings on the walls of subterranean caves, he somehow managed to look just as he must have looked in 1917: hardly a day older. Perhaps a better simile to indicate the effect of remoteness he gave, standing there with a vacant expression and both hands in his pockets, would be that of some rare insect enclosed in amber. He wore a minute Charlie Chaplin moustache, his dark, shiny hair, in which there was a touch of red, rolling away from his forehead like the stone locks of a sculpted head of Caracalla. (1)

The insect shows that size is irrelevant, remoteness in time the point. Although 1917 is less than twenty years ago, 'one' could only have seen him 'live' in one's earliest schooldays, millennia ago. How he has achieved this effect is mysterious and funny. 'Slow motion' is a term sometimes applied to Powell's writing: 'subterranean' insists on the right to full enjoyment of the analogy, the chill remoteness of the caves. Language abolishes history in reflections such as these – Ted is Chaplin and Caracalla; and it is so throughout *Dance*. Boys at school are migrating tribes, nomads of the steppe and so are Tess of Le Touquet and Di in her collar and tie. St John Clarke's secretaries, before the age of Members and Quiggin, are 'a line whose names, like those of prehistoric kings, had not survived, or at best were to be met with only in the garbled forms of popular legend, in this case emanating from the accumulated conflux of St John Clarke myth propagated by Members and Quiggin'. It may be that Clarke will have left his money to the Communist party, 'like a robber baron endowing the Church with his lands' (*Casanova's Chinese Restaurant*, 4). All literature as well as all history is available for the unhurried, meticulously phrased reflection on life (especially people). Jenkins especially likes to multiply incongruous details, all supported by a single point of analogy. Gwatkin looks shocked when Jenkins suggests that he might seduce the barmaid Maureen.

> He looked at me astonished. I felt a shade uncomfortable, rather like Mephistopheles unexpectedly receiving a hopelessly negative reaction from Faust. Such an incident in opera, I thought, might suggest a good basis for an *aria*. (*The Valley of Bones*, 4)

The narrator's voice is often close, as it is here, to Moreland's. Social circumstance is equally attractive to Jenkins. He records, as Stringham would have passed on, the detail about hospitality at Dogdene, a house so grand that it is almost impenetrable, under Geoffrey, Marquess of Sleaford, Chips's 'second Sleaford uncle': '"Shepherd's pie for luncheon," Lovell said, "and not enough sprouts"' (*At Lady Molly's*, 5). He researches the pasts of houses and families, 'finding' the fictional Dogdene in Pepys and an earlier Erridge in Creevey's memoirs. His voice can be as academically careful (scornful of Sillery's claims to scholarship) as those of Pennistone and Emily Brightman: 'Boadicea – Budicca, one would name her, if speaking with Dr Brightman' (*Temporary Kings*, 6).

Long sentences are characteristic, increasingly elliptical in the later volumes, relatives and articles omitted, phrases added in parenthesis, grammar sometimes sacrificed to the urge to juxtapose as many impressions, analogies, qualifications, hypotheses as possible, overburdened sentences occasionally suggesting that Latin might have suited Jenkins better. More often, in long sentences, there is a sprightliness and energy about the elaborate writing, and a redeeming sense of amusement at the laborious nature of language, given thought's speed. Short sentences can be as pungent as any in Kingsley Amis (a writer often reminiscent of Powell). Bernard Shernmaker is told at the Donners Dinner that the Quiggin girls are on their way. 'Shernmaker's face contorted horribly. Nightmares of boredom and melancholy oozed from him, infecting all the social atmosphere round about. Somebody put a drink in his hand. Tension relaxed a little' (*Hearing Secret Harmonies*, 3).

The skilled timing of short sentences makes the most of General

Liddament on Trollope, quoted above. The last word in the picture of Shernmaker is typical of the quiet force Powell gives his narrator. Meeting Sir Gavin in *The Acceptance World*, Jenkins says: 'He looked no older; perhaps a shade less sane' (4). A key word that seems exactly right constantly impresses the reader. Truscott disregards undergraduate opinion, all equally 'inchoate substance' (*A Question of Upbringing*, 4). Truscott regards Miss Walpole-Wilson as a challenge to his conversational powers because her personality 'provides intractable material'; Sir Gavin says that he is no medievalist and then glares about, perhaps as though he expects to be accused of 'covert' medievalism (*A Buyer's Market*, 3). Such hypotheses, usually introduced 'as if', are typical of the narrative. St John Clarke speaks of the Spanish Civil War 'as if' it were being arranged for his personal benefit (*Casanova's Chinese Restaurant*, 2). No sympathetic reader can listen to the narrator for long without amusement. The narrator's darker aphorisms are thoughtfully sad, not gloomy in a negative sense. V. S. Pritchett, craftsman in melancholy prose, chose two from the last chapter of *Casanova's Chinese Restaurant* in his review. Moreland cannot easily find words to cheer up Maclintick: 'He also lacked that subjective, ruthless love of presiding over other people's affairs which often makes basically heartless people adept at offering effective consolation.' Maclintick's suicide puts an end to Moreland's love of Priscilla: 'Love had received one of those shattering jolts to which it is peculiarly vulnerable from extraneous circumstance.' Pritchett praised the writing as 'melancholy, sane, experienced' and without cynicism.

> His epigrams are withering but they do not utterly demolish. Their balance is as belligerent as their wit. . . . He has a sense of proportion, yet he also has edge. It is an uncommon pair of gifts. [The second quotation] contains, down to the very word 'peculiarly', undertones and overtones of this novelist, in whose work the human comedy is grimly engrained.[53]

We are constantly reminded of the unsympathetic reader, by the voice of Widmerpool. He is, rather, the non-reader who could hear no overtones or undertones, no fun or sadness. His clichés and formulas, fluent and energetic from start to finish, imply the speaker's deafness to what is human in all voices but his own. 'Your joke is no doubt very amusing', he says to Jenkins at the *Fission* party. The saddest aspect of his last days, when Furioso, is that he thinks he has freed himself from humbug. Delavacquerie reports his reply to the Donners Prize committee's query about Gwinnett's book on Trapnel: 'Lord Widmerpool informed me straightaway that he did not care a fart – that was his unexpected phrase – what was said about him in Professor Gwinnett's book . . . as he held all contemporary writings of our day in hearty contempt' (*Hearing Secret Harmonies*, 3). The word 'hearty' in that setting is Widmerpool's typical note. We cannot feel very sorry for him, because he is damned by his own proclamations. However disagreeable what he has to say, furthermore, there is usually some mirth of which he is unaware ingrained in it.

6
Conclusions

X. Trapnel, most argumentative of the novelists in the cast of *Dance*, has much to say about the nature of fiction, and some of his remarks seem to have the author's approval. Jenkins remembers him saying (in *Books Do Furnish a Room*, 3) that 'a novelist writes what he is', repeating it on the last page of the same volume: 'a novel is what its writer is', Jenkins adding that 'the definition opens up a lot more questions'; he quotes it again in the final volume (2). Powell told an interviewer, while still working on the sequence, that 'the novel is not what you make but what you are'.[54] Trapnel's original assertion was that the subject matter – medieval romance or moon journey – is unimportant: the approach to life is what matters. Because Jenkins so closely reflects his author, one of the questions opened up, if we use Trapnel's thought as a starting-point, concerns the first-person narrative.

Much of the Dance is the work of Jenkins's imagination and sense of humour, so that we can think of Time and his music as metaphorical rather than metaphysical terms. The *Boyhood of Cyrus* dances through the sequence because Jenkins is amused by the odd way in which the picture has taken his fancy; he makes a dance out of words such as 'amaranth' (in Clarke's title and Belgian breeches), and voices such as Moreland's mimicking Sir Magnus Donners, which can drive 'fissures' through 'variegated seams of Time'. Time himself is made to dance to Jenkins's music – often in passages inspired by the pictures of the old man, Poussin's and others. Moreland's 'Beethoven-shaped' head sometimes resembles (although 'more intellectual') that of the infant Folly in Bronzino's painting (*An Allegory*, in the National Gallery, London) of Venus, Cupid, Folly and Time, where 'Time in the background, whiskered like the Emperor Franz-Josef, looms behind a blue curtain as if evasively vacating the bathroom' (*Casanova's Chinese Restaurant*, 1). Time dances to another tune in the statuette *Truth Unveiled by Time*, doomed to appear and reappear with the passage of fiction – and to be sneered at by Lord Huntercombe. Nicolas Poussin's painting *A Dance to the Music of Time*, not named but described in the second paragraph of the first volume, is referred to again in *Hearing Secret Harmonies* where it is said that Ariosto's Time 'although equally hoary and naked ... [is] not Poussin's Time ... in the picture where the Seasons dance':

> Poussin's Time (a painter's Time) is shown in a sufficiently unhurried frame of mind to be sitting down while he strums his instrument. The smile might be thought a trifle sinister, nevertheless the mood is genial, composed. (2)

Here the Poussin takes its place in the vast assembly of myths and voices which Nicholas (coincidentally) Jenkins has assembled. It comes as an almost careless allusion in the course of a long meditation on Ariosto, but Poussin's leisured Time – unlike the frantically hurried figure in the epic – joins the other Times in the mythology, so that the picture that gives the novel its title seems not a piece of literary scaffolding (as has sometimes been said) but possessed of a properly comic role in the narrator's scheme of things. In all such regions of the novel, the Dance and the music are 'immanent': Jenkins's creation, with no transcendental implications about the nature of things.

Powell chose to insist that they are transcendental: if we believe Jenkins's story, we must accept that Canon Fenneau's words are to be taken seriously: 'May I say that you bear out a deeply held conviction of mine as to the repetitive contacts of certain souls in the earthly lives of other individual souls.' Midway in the final volume (4), how can Jenkins disagree? Powell might have decided to make his narrator responsible for the seemingly overwhelming operation of coincidence, a character with a taint of Trelawneyism in his otherwise very upright mind, always hankering after 'magic in action', the Doctor's phrase for chance. In this way, all aspects of the Dance could have been kept within his realm, the comings and goings of the cast dance-like only as a result of his power of narrative choice. The highly selective reporting of the life – one week of childhood, two days of school, a few parties out of all the early London years – would have suited such a treatment, and the restricted social circles where people do keep meeting one another could have been used to rationalise the coincidences, and to show us that Jenkins, not Time, had put the extraordinary patterning into the account of his life. On the contrary, Powell takes responsibility for what Time has done. Jenkins tells us that his dedicated writer's life keeps him out of society for long spells, not worth reporting: whenever he does leave home, he meets Widmerpool and the rest of the cast wherever he goes. He tends to be sceptical about 'magic in action', trying to explain away, for example, the seeming reference to Murtlock in Ariosto. Reflecting in *The Kindly Ones* (3) on the sudden reappearance of Duport (which has 'cut a savage incision across Time'), 'I was bound to him throughout eternity', he is, as usual, speaking metaphorically. Because of his affair with Jean, Duport is 'part of [his] life' and can never be forgotten, however disagreeable. Behind this passage and very many others, however, there is implied an author who takes the words literally and holds that Jenkins is bound to keep meeting Duport, as he is bound to meet and remeet Widmerpool. Mrs Erdleigh, the novel and therefore the author says, is right to think that all our meetings are written in the stars and, sometimes, in a wicked pack of cards.

We can, of course, enjoy the sequence without believing anything of the kind. In so far as the story compels us, by the art of its telling, to suspend our disbelief in all the odd chance happenings, and even more, wherever the comedy diverts our attention from the contriving (until we think back), Powell persuades us to live with his belief for the sake of all the interest and pleasure the novel yields. We accept coincidence as a convention in many kinds of fiction. Powell has had to create his own convention: myriad coincidence. He does devote considerable narrative skill to carrying it off. Bold moves such as the placing of Widmerpool in the DAAG's chair at the end of *The Valley of Bones*, and Bithel's attachment to Murtlock's band, work because they are so bold, defying us to say that such chances cannot arise in life. The reappearance of the vague undergraduate Paul, in the background at Sillery's tea-party in the first volume, as Canon Fenneau in the last is a masterly stroke – surprising, apt and funny in the extent to which the shy young man has been completely metamorphosed by Time. Comedy often justifies unlikely congregations of Powell's people, as it does when Duport, Trelawney and Mrs Erdleigh assemble with Jenkins and Albert at the Bellevue. David Pennistone, met on a train in *The Valley of Bones*, turns out to be the young man with the orchid at Milly Andriadis's party in *A Buyer's Market*; he and Jenkins turn this into a joke and agree to meet again by force of will. When they achieve this, at the interview with Finn in the next volume, the comic pattern demands that Jenkins join the military philosophers in spite of the weakness of his French. Where the humour thins, however, or if the story flags, Powell's contrivance rubs through the texture: the rather humdrum joy-ride in *A Question of Upbringing* assembles in one car Jean's brother Templer, Duport who will marry her, and Jenkins and Brent who will have affairs with her. This is not incredible in itself, but a rereading of the novel may make us wonder whether the scene was written for the sake of the coincidence, and resent, for once, Powell's design. Such instances, which diminish the interest of Jenkins's observations on the 'patterns of life', are few, given the extent to which all members of the cast coincide.

A few of the scenes where we see the magicians in action disturb the story by inartistically letting the author's hand show. When the planchette writes phrases from Marx, and otherwise teases Quiggin, in *The Acceptance World* (3), we know what he cannot: who is cheating. When Murtlock discovers telepathically where Mr Gauntlett's dog Daisy has got to in the first chapter of the last volume, it would have been artistically superior (without disproving his thaumaturgic power) for him to have been wrong. Miracles in the novels of Graham Greene have often the same illusion-breaking weakness. Fiction caves in under the impact of a second order of pretending. It does not matter that planchette-boards write mysteriously, or that some people have a sixth sense. Powell can interest us, in his memoirs, by telling a story of the uncanny from his own experience: Constant Lambert appeared to have telephoned from beyond the grave.[55] He could not successfully put such a thing into a novel. On the rare occasions when he tries, playing tricks on his narrator, he lets the novel show 'what he is', that is to say, show his conception of life, in the wrong sort of way.

The right way prevails throughout *Dance*, however, and among the 'mages' appears best in Mrs Erdleigh, a wonderful creation. Scorpio Murtlock is the least successful, perhaps because he is quite outside the comedy where she, Trelawney and Canon Fenneau have their being. Powell's wish to make him sinister often leaves his occult expressions sounding flat and banal. Doctor Trelawney is like Fenneau, a caricature; and we cannot take seriously a magician who gets locked in a bathroom. Such an indignity is not to be imagined in the case of Mrs Erdleigh who floats across carpets, managing her 'swirl of capes, hoods, stoles, scarves, veils' to superbly 'spectral effect', partly by professionalism, partly by massive will-power, and perhaps (his sense of propriety obliges Jenkins to acknowledge) by powers not to be explained. She is a far better talker than Murtlock, her flood of occult quotation and social observation poised between poetry and farce, and her talk combines with her stagily ethereal 'presence' to command respect. Courtesy plays a crucial part in Jenkins's dealings with her. He verges on the shocking *faux pas*, when referring to Dr Trelawney's end, in *Temporary Kings* (5), of mentioning death. She saves him from the lapse:

'You mean not long before he achieved the Eighth Sphere to which Trismegistus refers?'
'Exactly.'
'Where, as again Vaughan writes, the liberated soul ascends, looking at the sunset towards the west wind, and hearing secret harmonies . . .'

She is not surprised to hear that Emily Brightman mentioned Thomas Vaughan when they were all in Venice: 'His spirit was moving there'. Thomas Vaughan ('Eugenius Philalethes, as we know him') calls the body the 'green lion', an obvious symbolic connection, she thinks, with the lion of St Mark. When she speaks of Vaughan and Hermes Trismegistus, she ponders life's eternal foundations, plumbed by these great alchemists but quite unknown, she observes, to Baby Wentworth or Pamela Widmerpool. In talk of this kind she is, like Jenkins, a myth-maker, with a comic role in the novel's most imaginative realms. Planchette and telepathy belong to a lower order of fiction, one less likely to persuade us that the Dance has a transcendental background in the world of light.

X. Trapnel's talk reflects Powell's views in what he says about 'naturalism'.[56] 'You just look round at what's happening and shove it down', he says, summarising with scorn the naïve misconception of novel-writing to be found among politically minded people such as Books Bagshaw. He prefers 'naturalism' to 'realism' because it is free of the old delusion that a novelist copies 'the real world'. Naturalism is 'just as selective and artificial as if the characters were kings and queens speaking in blank verse', he tells Bagshaw (*Books Do Furnish a Room*, 5). A tape-recording of a slice of life 'wouldn't come out as it should' because most actual talk is too disorganised and boring for fiction. But although he makes his characters better speakers than their flesh-and-blood counterparts, he aims to make his novels lifelike. Naturalism can only be lifelike, he says, if the writer is good enough. Bagshaw is wrong to think that Tolstoy is 'like' life (Trapnel always keeps quotation marks round 'like') because he is naturalistic: he is 'like' life because his naturalism is so good. Dostoevsky and Dickens can be as lifelike as Tolstoy is, in un-naturalistic modes. Trapnel sounds distinctly Powellian in his examples (citing Petronius, Powell's favourite ancient author), and in saying that when life sometimes achieves naturalistic 'happenings', these appear in 'grotesque, irrational trivialities'.

Powell has told an interviewer that naturalism is a proper term for his work and that he aims to write well enough to make it lifelike. Powell's generation, which followed the Modernists (Conrad, Joyce, Woolf, Firbank), included Evelyn Waugh (born 1903), Christopher Isherwood(1904), Graham Greene (1904) and Henry Green (1905). They saw that the Modernist experiments with techniques had divorced twentieth-century fiction from the practice of the Victorians, which survived, Powell thought, only in such spent forces as St John Clarke. Modernist terms appear in some of Jenkins's strictures on Clarke, condemned for, 'so I had come to think, the emptiness of the writing's inner content' (*A Buyer's Market*, 4). They did not wish, however, to seem Joycean or Woolfian, or to sacrifice to experiment, story-telling or 'life' in the sense of human behaviour in English society. The concept of an artificial, selective naturalism, aiming to be lifelike by force of the writing's quality but sceptical about 'the real world', caters for two impulses in Powell, and perhaps in some of his contemporaries. He is a Post-Modernist, but writing in the same genre as Tolstoy.

Marcel Proust is the Modernist with whom Powell invites the most obvious, although superficial, comparison. *A la recherche du temps perdu* is a sequence-novel narrated in the first person by a narrator who moves in high society and among artistic people, full of thoughts about memory and Time. Reading *Dance*, however, is a very different experience. Proust's Marcel is far more introspective than Jenkins, always exploring the inner world of self while Jenkins guards much of his private experience, even his childhood memories being mostly of other people. *The Military Philosophers* is closest to a Proustian supplanting of the outer world with the more vivid reality in one's own mind, but this is uncharacteristic and Jenkins's mind is chiefly filled with his reading (including Proust). *Dance* has no equivalent, either, to Proust's distinction between deliberate (unsatisfactory) remembering and involuntary memory of the kind induced by the little cake soaked in tea, the *madeleine*, which re-creates the Combrai of Marcel's childhood. Time and memory are not philosophical problems to Jenkins as they are to Marcel. He is a less theoretical (perhaps therefore more English) intellectual. Powell's reading of Proust at Oxford must, none the less, have contributed to his discovery, confirmed by many other modern writers, including Ronald Firbank, that novels could be free from the cumbersome Victorian plots, and as free from chronicling, in chronological order, as our memories are. Proust must also have encouraged him, although this is more apparent in *Dance* than in the prewar novels, in developing the poetic possibilities of the furnishings of the mind. Proust may have taught him the comic possibilities of abrupt narrative interruptions and prolonged digressions, although this might have been learned, equally well, within the English tradition, from Laurence Sterne's *Tristram Shandy* (1759–67), a book showing that a novelist who writes well enough can produce entertainment from every kind of narrative order and disorder.

Some critics have presented Powell as a Post-Modernist, his work quite unlike nineteenth-century fiction. Peter Conrad, for example, argues that Jenkins's world is 'a fading mirage' rather than 'a solidifying of society, like the chronicles of Trollope or Balzac'. Quoting Trapnel's idea that 'a novelist's like a fortune-teller', and saying that 'for Powell the novel's powers are unearthly', Conrad emphasises those aspects of *Dance* in which Jenkins's imagination works magic with events, and Jenkins and other characters 'commune with' the literature of the past. In such an account Jenkins is a magician summoning up charades from the past, against a chorus of ghostly commentators speaking from old books. He is, in this view, a narrator, not a character, a literary voice that mimics other voices but cannot know other characters, having no last word of his own but returning, in the long quotation from Burton that ends the sequence, into the literature from which he has been made.

This is one way of explaining what the sequence is like: it establishes how Powell differs from Trollope and Balzac, and helps to show why readers have called *Dance* 'a poem', resembling in its images, voices and quotations a vastly expanded prose equivalent to *The Waste Land*. Readings of this kind have the advantage of freeing us from false expectations: that the novel ought to give a complete picture of twentieth-century English society, for example. Conrad's interpretation takes no account, however, of the impression of many readers that *Dance* is true to life.[57] The reviewer of *Temporary Kings* for *The Times Literary Supplement* concluded:

> The fineness of Mr Powell's art, the near genius of his sense of design, consists in his ability to conceive and render believable in 'fiction' the sheer multifariousness of real human experience in his age. Reputations founded on inventions less true and more feigning begin to wane almost irrecoverably in the light of his achievement.

The same (anonymous) reviewer offers a summing-up of Powell which could be called classical: 'as always the novel ultimately pivots on a concept of the profound comedy of all human postures and strivings'.[58] That is an alternative to Conrad's explanation of the sequence, and it is also convincing.

It would be odd to talk about Powell for long without praising his characters. Although Jenkins is always sceptical about his knowledge of other people, gathering gossip like a second Aubrey – as Conrad notes – and often amused by the difficulty of saying what one's friends and acquaintances are like, he brings them so vividly to life that we share his insatiable curiosity to know more. We know his people (like real ones) imperfectly but we can form judgments about many of them with as much confidence as those we have to form in life: we would trust General Conyers in the direst crisis; we would not trust Dr Trelawney at all. *The Times Literary Supplement*'s reviewer exaggerates the extent of Powell's knowledge of contemporary life. He has wisely restricted himself to the sort of people he has known. He achieves more with those whose social backgrounds and early lives he can imagine from his own experience: Moreland can talk about his childhood; Quiggin and Members cannot – although Powell makes a small comedy of the 'obscurity' of their background.

He is even more restricted in his ability to portray women. Intellectuals such as Ada Leintwardine and Emily Brightman are successful, but only in scenes, at literary committees and conferences, where they talk in the erudite gossipy manner of Jenkins's male friends. Maltilda is among the more interesting women, but her talk becomes stiff and effortful when she talks about her emotional life. Jenkins can speculate about even such an enigmatic man as Gwinnett but he has no inkling of what Pamela might be like. She is given little to say and her remarks often sound borrowed from other writers. 'I warned her that old fool Craggs, whose firm she's joining, is as randy as a stoat. I threw a glass of Algerian wine over him once when he was trying to rape me. Christ, his wife's a bore' (*Temporary Kings*, 2). This, Pamela at her liveliest, sounds like a voice from the more stylised, fantastical world of Simon Raven's sequence, *Alms for Oblivion*. The dry, intelligent voice of Lady Isobel, heard rarely and briefly, reminds us that omission of Jenkins's marriage, beyond the need to be justified in so far as he is a Post-Modernist narrator, is a shortcoming if we think of the sequence in terms of the multifariousness of experience.

The claim of truth-to-life implies the possibility of a framework of ideas and here Powell certainly has nothing original to offer. The sequence has no answers to ultimate questions and seems especially evasive about the question of evil. Are Pamela and Widmerpool demonic creatures, clawing at each other because they are possessed by evil, or are they just painfully unhappy people? Is Scorpio Murtlock a diabolical or merely a nasty young man? The ambiguity is most awkward in Pamela's case; she is a child of hell, Mrs Erdleigh and others imply, while Emily Brightman speaks indulgently of her 'naughtinesses'. Widmerpool is by far the most lifelike of this threesome who seem to have an evil dimension that Powell is in two minds about, and, in his self-destructive quest for power, can be seen as a representative villain of our time. Jenkins very frequently remarks on the awful driving force of the egoistic greed for power – a Stendhalian theme present since the earliest novels – and he seems to link it with his strictures on the left, but he draws no conclusions. Powell might say that the hope for such results is a nineteenth-century misconception: that we do not read fiction for definite answers to the questions life poses, and he might add that a novelist's values are ingrained in everything he writes, that he writes what he is. It could be argued that the victory of Jenkins over Widmerpool is only a new treatment of the traditional English victory of gentleman over cad. Jenkins might reasonably object that he presents himself in various roles: one is also an intellectual and an artist, with friends including Barnby and Trapnel who would scoff at the term 'gentleman'; he is also a soldier, for a time, with Bithel as a comrade in arms. Widmerpool is never quite that, nor a schoolfellow, nor a friend, nor, it appears, a husband. It is in his genius for avoiding all the best relationships life offers that Widmerpool, the most stupendous cad in English literature, seems a characterisation of Russian subtlety and thoroughness of presentation.

'Reading novels needs almost as much talent as writing them' is another of Trapnel's precepts, recollected by Jenkins in *Temporary Kings* (4). Reading *Dance*, we must negotiate with different sets of expectations: some Post-Modernist, appropriate in reading, for example, Vladimir Nabokov; others, if we share them with *The Times Literary Supplement* reviewer who wrote of truth to life in Powell's less feigning inventions, which we bring to Kingsley Amis or V. S. Naipaul. A more Nabokovian *Dance* (closer to the Nabokov of *Ada*), if we try to imagine such a novel, might have been more rigidly consistent, and more elaborately playful ('ludic'), with the fictional nature of Jenkins's world. By Nabokovian standards it is a mistake for the narrator never to have heard of the fictional Tiepolo in Jacky Bragadin's palace, and for him to tell us that Bragadin will not allow it to be photographed, as though protecting it from our scepticism: in the world of Deacons, Isbisters and Tokenhouses, Tiepolo's *Candaules and Gyges* ought to be world-famous. It is, on the same sort of reading, a flaw for Le Bas to name Balliol (in *A Question of Upbringing*, 4) since no other college is mentioned, 'the university' is (like 'school') never named, and language peculiar to Oxford (such as scout for college-servant) is avoided. In Nabokov the 'fictiveness' of the work is complete, self-contained and part of the comedy. That is not so in *Dance*; for all its imaginary places, books and paintings, it is, unlike *Ada*, so lived in, so close to the author's experience of the corresponding institutions in our world and able to convey the feel of them, that even its purely fictional elements seem 'real': Kingsley Amis wrote that 'one could hardly credit not having come across Mr Deacon's *Boyhood of Cyprus* ... in some municipal gallery'.[59] Trapnel toys with the idea that everything in a novel is 'true', on the grounds, although he does not say so, of Sir Philip Sidney's view that the poet ever lies and therefore never feigns. Powell may have had that purist approach in mind when he quotes Sir Thomas Browne's 'Some Truths seem almost Falsehoods and some Falsehoods almost Truths', adding that these words 'contain in a sense the justification of all novel writing'.[60] There is always another sense, however, in a mixed kind of fiction: poetic and naturalistic. Powell has always wanted to write well enough to be lifelike.

The difficulty of explaining literature's dealings with life is a theme in the two novels of the 1980s. In *O, How the Wheel Becomes It!* (1983) and *The Fisher King* (1986), Powell almost comes to see man as *Homo narrans*, a story-telling animal, for whom political, social and sexual life exist only for the sake of tales to be told. But he does not seem even tempted by the view that life is entirely made up of fictions, or that all fictions are equal. The first book treats myth as a refuge from experience – myth in the negative sense of Widmerpool's urge 'to get on'; in the second, myth-making is a creative and comic rendering of experience. Both novels assert that life weaves stories in which we have to play our parts, and can break through our myth-making with painful blows.

O, How the Wheel Becomes It! turns on the discovery of a diary, good enough to count as literature, and threateningly true to life. Half a century ago, two old schoolfellows G. F. H. Shadbold and Cedric Winterwade were rivals in letters and in love. Both loved Isolde Upjohn, who was infinitely slender and looked like a cover for *Vogue*. Shadbold thought himself the more likely to succeed. He also looked down on Winterwade's intellectual pretensions, and was briefly alarmed when his friend's attempt at a best-seller, *The Welsons of Omdurman Terrace*, seemed about to 'take wing', while his own advanced, austere writings were largely ignored. That did not happen. Winterwade had not published another book when he was killed in the war. Now a publisher has asked Shadbold to report on and perhaps edit Winterwade's diary. He finds that the talent for ironic observation that failed to show itself in *The Welsons* went into the diary, which is worryingly good. Worse follows. Decoding the diary's symbols, Shadbold finds that Winterwade, although briefly and ingloriously, was the lover of Isolde Upjohn, having taken her, for a weekend, to Paris. He is particularly infuriated because the diary's frankness concerning the 'less than idyllic' sexual bouts with Isolde at the Hotel Bouguereau has the painful ring of truth.

> Life's way – anyway Love's way – always possessed lights and shadows, the shadows as often as not predominating. Winterwade acknowledged that fact with amused resignation. Shadbold found philosophic appreciation of this truth, Winterwade's pitiless transcription of the episode's ups and downs, obnoxious in the extreme. If Winterwade had indulged in transports of bogus delight, Shadbold could more easily have dismissed the descriptions as fictitious. An uncompromising realism was even more offensive to a literary critic of his own acknowledged standing. (5)

Life and letters have become vexatiously mixed up, and the complications of the comedy that follows mix them up further. Shadbold's literary jealousy revives. Full of lively revelations about the 1920s, the diary could make Winterwade better known than himself. Sexual jealousy hurts even more. Shadbold has been injured in his personal myth: 'one whole facet of memory had been dislocated'. He has preserved and cherished an 'image' of Isolde. The fact that he was one of many young men who pursued her in vain, and that she was 'kept' by an older, richer man somewhere in the background, has not troubled him. There has until now been no 'recorded physical connection with a man known to him personally'; connection with Winterwade is worst of all. The thought is not to be borne: 'the desecration of myth was something not to be condoned in any circumstances' (6). The screw twists once more on Shadbold's self-esteem because the diary covers the 1939–45 war, an 'episode' he has persuaded himself to be mostly fictional, exaggerated in the writings of those who, unlike him, took part in it. He reports that the diary is not worth publishing.

Life now punishes him for suppressing literature. It does so by inflicting on him a form of torment by narrative: wherever he goes he has to hear or tell Winterwade's story. He is the more susceptible because guilt adds to the pain of desecrated myth: he was once a Zouch-like Superman, completely unscrupulous; but age has weakened his will. He hopes to bury both guilty secret and tarnished image, but everyone suddenly becomes inquisitive about Winterwade. One of his wife's former husbands, an 'Englit don' called Grigham, has become interested in *The Welsons*, 'struck by the total oblivion into which the book has fallen' (8), and means to do research. Then comes a visit from Isolde. Many times married, at present Mrs Abdullah, she has created her own myth of Winterwade as a great man and a war-hero. Arriving on the day Shadbold is to be interviewed for television by the dreadful Rod Cubbage, she joins the programme and turns it into a Winterwade Show. She and Cubbage bully Shadbold into saying he admires *The Welsons* and envies its author's heroic death. He half-agrees to write the Introduction to the memoirs of Mrs Abdullah. Later, his wife has to be told. 'Shadbold sighed. There was a long pause. Then Prudence Shadbold began all over again. The saga of the Cubbage shooting had once more to be rehashed' (18). His one remaining solace, the fact that the diary's existence is a secret, is destroyed when Prudence tells Grigham about it, firing him with enthusiasm for further research. Fan-letters after the Cubbage broadcast all 'sting' Shadbold in one way or another. The local publican, obnoxious to Shadbold, was Winterwade's comrade in the army, and has made his own myth. The *coup de grace* is his hearing that Winterwade's son, believing the diary worthless, has destroyed it. Mrs Abdullah attends the funeral. Death has spared Shadbold, it seems, from having to talk about his old friend indefinitely.

Literature's dealings with life are comic in other ways: one is the narrative method. This short book, which the title-page calls 'a novel' (forbidding 'novella'), is for Powell crowded with incidents, and the point of view is unobtrusive. The narrator is tarter than Jenkins, although sharing some features of his thought and style. He acts as reporter and editor of a story developed by Jason Price, the young publisher who handles the diary. Responsibility for 'ominiscient' passages, where nobody could know what was in Shadbold's mind, is shuffled onto Price who has 'imaginatively improved' on his story by inventing them, in telling the tale to friends, and elaborating the 'saga'. For Price, the 1920s, like the 1890s, are utterly remote, legendary epochs, a view reflected in the narrator's metaphors which, like those of *Dance*, insist on distancing such relatively recent periods, in the mind's eye: 'in the late 1920s – to use the phraseology of carbon-dating – give or take a hundred years' (2); 'Back in that paleolithic age' (3). Remoteness turns saga into myth. Obsessed with the 1920s and the 1890s, Price fills his conversation with their literary and social legends and lore ('Ernest Dowson remarked that absinthe makes the tart grow fonder', 4), and the narrator borrows his style. Isolde is very well-preserved, and therefore 'in Jason Price's terms again a positive Dorian Gray of the female sex' (13). Price glamorises his favourite periods, speaking of them as 'decades of intoxicating women and intoxicated men dancing a pavan through lost kingdoms of Cockayne' (4). These myths fed by literature, as well as the private inventions of Isolde and the publican, are undermined by what the diary tells about life, and especially of the unromantic 1920s weekend on the hard beds of the Hotel Bouguereau.

Life defeats literature in the subplot which concerns Prudence Shadbold. An author of detective stories, she plans to update the genre with *Culture-Code of Samphire*, the adventures of a homosexual youth who murders a professor at a new university: the youth is known as 'Samphire' among the academic staff because he is 'dreadful trade' (after *King Lear*, IV. v. 15). Shadbold warns her against visiting Grigham at his campus, lest her plot prove too close to circumstances there, which turns out to be the case: 'all the most sinister and perverse acts I'd thought up are the daily life of this academic backwater', she complains (17). Her book has to be rewritten. A related joke is the badness of Westerwade's novel, on which Shadbold reflects as damningly as Jenkins brooded on St John Clarke, and its academic acceptability today. Grigham is a satirical skit on jargon-ridden professors of English: he says he is making 'a survey into the insightful fiction' of the 1920s; he is well aware that 'the author is merely a nodal bond', and he finds in *The Welsons* 'unexpected culture-codes and utterance-types' (8).

Powell's ear for utterance-types is as sharp as ever in the dialogue of this novel and he finds new types in Cubbage's television style and in the speech of the landlord of the pub, Major Jock Crowter, whose talk assembles a remarkable collection of present-day middle-class-British English vulgarisms. Powell's instinct for characters' names is also as sure as in the sequence (although here they are much closer to farce), and so is his flair for imaginary book-titles: Shadwell's two novels were *Trip the Pert Fairies*, and *Thumbs*, 'described in reviews as "experimental"'. The words of his own title are Ophelia's (*Hamlet*, IV. v. 172), and the wheel is Fortunes's.

The Fisher King presents an attempt to enrich life by myth-making and shows life's power to surprise the myth-maker. The story is set on the cruise-ship *Alecto*, on a holiday voyage round the British Isles. The central figures, Saul Henchman and Barberina Rookwood, are a characteristically Powellian pair since he is a man of indomitable will-power, and she, a ballerina of the highest order, an artist. Power and art are not completely separated in this pairing, however, since he is exceptionally talented in the ambiguous (perhaps 'bastard') art of photography, while she has considerable will-power of her own. Henchman needs to be determined, having been very badly disabled in the war; unlike most of Powell's power-loving characters, he combines this urge with intelligence, imagination and a sense of humour. Asked in a radio interview what book he would want to have with him if shipwrecked on a desert-island, he names Stendhal's *Armance*:

'His first and unfinished novel, as you probably remember. Not one of his best, but as it deals with the problems of an impotent man . . .'

'Ah, yes,' said the interviewer. 'And thank you, Saul Henchman.'

Although ugly, and known for his rudeness, he has won Barberina's devotion; she has sacrificed her career to look after him (while keeping up her daily practice). Some see 'an icy inner loneliness' (23), and think her 'a nun of art' (14). Another idea about this unusual relationship is that 'Henchman's colossal self-esteem may have required the suppression of a great artist' (19).

That theory belongs to Valentine Beals, whose relation to the narrator resembles that of Jason Price in the earlier novel. Beals is another of Powell's bad-novelists, but he is a good bad-novelist, skilful at the craft of popular historical fiction, and certain that it is no more than a craft. He feels frustrated, however, by having to simplify all the characters and incidents in his books, and remorselessly exclude intelligence and imagination, since these qualities – even 'eroticism of too intellectual a tone' – are bad for business. He compensates in his 'hobby' of finding 'archetypes' for the people he meets. Some are appropriate for his own fiction. Dr Lorna Tiptoft, a strong-willed woman, might be the She-Wolf of France or Sarah, Duchess of Marlborough. Gary Lamont, a 'rising newspaper tycoon', is a Victorian office-boy asking for an increase in wages with confidence because he knows something bad about the boss. Other roles are from literature. Lamont is also Scott Fitzgerald's Gatsby (2). Mr Jack, elderly drunk and formidable bore, is a male Scheherazade, or the Ancient Mariner, or, since his stories are all about women, Don Juan (20). The more incongruous such roles the better, given a valid point of comparison. This very Powellian game is akin to Jenkins's myth-making, although Beals has to confine himself to conversation. *The Fisher King*'s narrator joins in, with images from the visual arts. Beals's dark complexion and 'opulent' shirts make him a quattrocento magnate, who ought to be pictured kneeling in the corner of an old master, pointing to Henchman as though to 'the paramount figure'. Beals would probably accept this image; he might wish Barberina to have a canvas to herself, one belonging to a different school, symbolising 'Love, Fame, Chastity, Sacrifice, Dissimulation, Betrayal, Jealousy' – art historians would dispute the exact interpretation 'in pedantic controversy' (1).

It is Henchman who fascinates Beals. He is Banquo, because there is 'no speculation in his eyes' (3). He is the Beast in relation to Barberina as Beauty (15). He is 'the Monkey', his nickname (a simian character, therefore, akin in Powell's world to Quiggin and Sillery). It is significant to Beals that he claims affinity, apropos of his Christian name, to King Saul of the Old Testament, rather than to the apostle who changed his name to Paul in the New, because this shows 'conscious acceptance of the royal dignity' (5). That supports Beals's basic theory about Henchman, that he is the Fisher King.

This 'misty personage' of Arthurian legend was impotent and crippled, and therefore reduced to fishing. Beals believes that Henchman fishes, so that he fills most demands of his archetype, although it is worrying that the Fisher King's lands were barren, while Henchman's photography business flourishes. Beals persuades his wife Louise and their old friends the Middlecotes to play the game of archetypes, testing their ingenuity. Henchman's nickname in the army was 'the Monkey' but this can be made to fit. 'The Monkey' arose from a vegetarian phase when Henchman would go to the Mess early and eat all the salads: he may have been under 'a ritual obligation', as the Fisher King, 'to abstain from flesh at certain seasons' (8). Arthurian roles can be found for other passengers: who is Perceval and who the Loathly Damsel? Fay Middlecote suggests that Barberina may be the maiden who bore the Cup, thought in the Middle Ages to be the Holy Grail, into the Fisher King's hall, when Perceval was feasting there. Alternatively, she might be 'a sort of female Perceval, who came to be photographed and didn't ask the right questions, so was forced to stay a prisoner in the castle'. Beals adds that dancing was a feature of fertility rites. Louise Beals thinks that Lorna Tiptoft is the Loathly Damsel, who came to Arthur's castle on a mule and bearing a scourge, to rebuke Perceval for his failure to ask the ritual questions about the Cup and the Spear which would have cured the King and made his lands fertile again.

A form of imaginary charades is possible when incidents offer Arthurian interpretations. When the ship's motion spills Henchman from his seat at the bar he is rescued by a young man called Robin Jilson. Jilson fetches his crutches and Middlecote hands them to Henchman.

> Beals described this procedure as manifesting a ceremony at the court of the Fisher King; a lesser courtier, in the shape of Jilson, not directly approaching the sovereign with the royal crutches, but presenting them through an intermediary of more august rank. (16)

This encounter leads to Henchman's patronising Jilson, a sickly young man who wants to become a photographer. The idea that Jilson may be Perceval is strengthened by the interest which Lorna Tiptoft takes in him.

The story-telling matters more than the incidents. One of the best scenes in the novel is a kind of battle of narrators. Beals is trapped, at dinner, between Mrs Jilson, an ardent fan who wants to discuss his novels, and Professor Kopf, an American specialist in Arthurian studies. Kopf overhears Mrs Jilson talking about Beals's *Lancelot's Love Feast*: 'But Mr Beals, I can never remember what Gawain did.' Unable to resist Arthurian debate, and desperate to escape narrative assault from his other neighbour, Mr Jack, he joins in (30). Beals has just broken off 'in the middle of an exposition, as circumspect as he could make it, of one of the more carnal passages in [his] Arthurian novel', one concerning 'the story about Gawain and the girl who was being boiled in a tub of water'. He notes that Gawain is less pure in the later stages of his career, more interested, for example, in the girl who carries the Cup, when he is allowed to see it, than in the Grail itself. Kopf intevenes to say that the girl was Elaine, niece or possibly daughter, from the time before he was maimed, of the Fisher King. Grateful to escape from Mrs Jilson, Beals is intrigued by this, to him, new aspect of the myth. But Professor Kopf is also demanding, at a different conversational level: 'You may have seen the current number of *The Bulletin of the Board of Celtic Studies*?' The Professor is spurred on to tell more Arthurian stories, however, by the threat of his other neighbour. 'Mr Jack was showing signs of wanting to break in to this conversation. He had begun to breathe heavily. Professor Kopf, noticing that, continued more desperately than ever.' He talks of King Lot, Gawain and Perceval. Beals fears that he may have bought 'temporary relief from Mrs Jilson' at a high price since Kopf means to lend him the latest number of the *Bulletin*, but he 'triumphs' when the Professor names the Fisher King in Henchman's presence. Henchman seizes on Kopf's saying that Perceval may have been a shaman, asking about 'medicine women', and Kopf then names the Loathly Damsel, his own special field. Beals is now convinced that Lorna Tiptoft must be the Damsel, who seems to be a counterpart to Henchman, moreover, by reversing (as the hideous crone Sir Perceval marries) the myth of Beauty and the Beast.

Beals's is a fashionable literary game, akin to those of Nabokov and John Barth, in playing Arthurian and contemporary concepts and language against each other. Perceval as a young man, too uncouth for admission to the Round Table, lacked 'the sort of chic required of an Arthurian knight', says Beals. He failed to ask the Fisher King the proper questions because he was wondering where to buy 'a suit of good cheap armour' or thinking that he would not want his girl's looks too Pre-Raphaelite, says Fay Middlecote (3). It is not confined to Beals's circle: Henchman plays too. Recalling the early 'Blue period', when he eked out his living by taking pornographic photographs, he pictures Mr

Jack arriving 'pillion' with the Loathly Damsel and her scourge, her mule attempting to manage the Soho stairs (31). Nor is it confined to Arthurian images, although these predominate. Henchman casts himself as Humpty Dumpty, liable to 'frequent tumbles, both physical and moral' (16). In Mr Jack, he sees Adam, 'not the sort of man one would care to have created oneself', because no woman could trust him (38). He broods on Poussin's *Les Bergers d'Arcadie*, where the shepherds of Arcadia find a tomb, reminding them that death rules even there. In the case of Jilson ET IN SUBURBIA EGO would be an appropriate inscription for the shepherd's tomb, he decides: death rules even in suburbia. Barberina imagines how he might have photographed Poussin's scene and he tells her that the shepherds of the picture might actually have been photographers, or 'a camera crew from Arcadia Television', as their beards and clothes imply (17).

Life is comic, also, to those who think about story-telling. *The Fisher King* is in a sense Beals's novel, and then again it is not, since he writes only in the genre of *Lancelot's Love Feast* and *Mistress to Maximus*. In the sense that the story of the *Alecto*'s cruise is constructed by Beals, and reported, from his talk, by Powell's narrator, it is provisional. Beals considers recasting it. Perhaps it should be Barberina's story rather than Henchman's. Perhaps 'things might have been reconstructed in terms of Tristram and Iseult' (39). Powell's narrator also broods on the narrative problems of presenting Henchman. Contradicting himself in all the ways Powell can invent, he even ponders whether, after all, Beals might have reworked Henchman and Barberina into an historical novel for the mass-market, and concludes that this would have been impossible, or, if possible and achieved, 'disastrous for sales' (18). He notes that Henchman fictionalises himself, accepting the analogy with the Beast loved by Beauty, certainly capable of telling his own story, with ironic panache, in terms of the Fisher King. He proves to be a formidable story-teller, subduing Mr Jack and Beals by out-narrating them with the tale of the Young King of the Black Isles from *The Arabian Nights*.

This further development in the narrative battles comes at an appropriate moment. However the story of the *Alecto*'s cruise is told, Beals maintains, it must pivot on the decision of Barberina Rookwood, who has fallen in love with Jilson, to leave Henchman. She has just made this apparent when Henchman tells the

Arabian story, and he is well situated, therefore, to embarrass Beals with its analogies. He talks with relish and in Powell's most astringent tones. The Young King's wife's lover

> was a Nubian slave who was also a leper and a paralytic. What we now call a deprived person. In the telling of the tale one can detect both lack of compassion and racial prejudice ... Physically unappealing lovers of beautiful women are a commonplace in Scheherazades's recital .... My own observation by no means divests that surmise of all credence. (33)

Beals is baffled, embarrassment aside, by the story's intended application. Is it, since the lover is dealt what would normally be a fatal blow by the Young King, and kept alive only by the power of the wife, a sorceress, a moral lesson for Mr Jack? Or, since the wife turns the Young King to stone from the navel down and lashes his back daily, does the tale refer to Henchman's sufferings? Does it merely show that there is no accounting for women's behaviour? Henchman's attributes seem divided between the Young King and the lover. Human life, the tale implies in this context – and Beals admits as much in the last chapter – does not accord neatly with archetypes.

In its myth-making and its narrative contests, the fiction can be considered artificial and cerebral, even poetic and abstract: Fay Middlecote asks Beals whether 'we haven't heard all this before from T. S. Eliot' (3). Poetry aside, so far as Beals's myth-making is concerned, all events have equal weight: Henchman's falling off his bar-stool and his losing Barberina signify only as raw material. There are scenes, however, where Beals's game is abandoned because it seems rebuked by events. In the best of these, Barberina dances before Henchman (and all those still on the *Alecto*'s dance floor) in salute and farewell, dumbfounding even Beals. He claims later, 'even when completely sober', that he cannot remember a moment in his life when he was so affected by a matter which did not directly concern him:

> It was something about their mutual recognition that the dance showed ritually that their relationship had come to an end. The absolute lack of any need for explanation, when something mattered so much. The horror that they were going to part hit me, too, as if below the belt. (34)

Beals has been turning Henchman's life into ritual in his game of archetypes. The novel asserts that life has brought Jilson, sickly enough to attract Barberina (although he chooses Lorna) and jolt her out of her relationship with Henchman, on this cruise, on a ship named for one of the Furies; and life has arranged for tonight's band to be playing pieces from *Swan Lake*, so that Barberina can stage her ritual in life. For a while, at least, the comic fantasy is dispelled. This scene is naturalistic. It is not presented as just one more narrative mode available to Beals, but as a rendering of the truth in human terms. Whether it is like life, according to Trapnel's criterion, depends on how good it is. The dramatic situation is strong, setting the claims of art and the world against those of the crippled old photographer. Barberina will dance again at Covent Garden, but he has been dealt a blow. The narrator has elsewhere distinguished between the tearful, glamorous terms proper for the situation in a Beals romance, and his own – drily comparing the relative steadiness of Henchman on crutches and Mr Jack after a session in the bar; saying that Barberina 'separated from Henchman, was now more or less on the open market' (33); generally granting both characters the dignity they deserve from rejection of self-pity, always a respectable stance in Powell. Henchman is usually sardonic, when not 'punitive', in speech, Barberina a gracious silence. Their 'ritual' parting, when she ends the dance, is moving because of the elimination of emotion elsewhere, and because emotional language is subdued here:

'The *pas seul* before the curtain?'
'If you like.'
'Naturally I feel a little sad.'
'Me . . .'
She did not, perhaps could not finish . . .

This is the moment that strikes Beals, 'as if below the belt'. 'Now you must be philosophical', she tells Henchman, after we have been reminded, by her asking if he is ready to be helped to bed, of his dependence; the narrator calls that 'a rather brutal phrase'. They are speaking in public, although they have ignored the bystanders. Pretending to make 'a regally dismissive gesture', Henchman turns the joke of Fisher King back upon Beals.

By the end of the story the conversational story-telling game has developed considerable poetic force. The final scene, on Orkney, where Henchman leaves the cruise to fish, attended only by Mr Jack, recalls the novel's opening sentence, 'Exile is the wound of kingship'. Barberina has exiled her Fisher King. The game might be thought of as the foreground of the book, funny, ingenious and in some respects modish: Powell has always liked to be up to date (and shows himself so in presenting the ad-man, Middlecote, as well as in remarks on the art, or craft of photography). Further back is the figure of Henchman (surrounded by his court, which notably includes Professor Kopf, a funny and sensitive addition to Powell's Americans and to his scholars), mythologically conceived but also naturalistically rendered as in Beals's 'full-dress' version of Barberina's dance, and, although psychologically inexplicable, psychologically very interesting as a discussion topic, for Beals and others. He is a far more solid figure than his archetype of legend. The novel's readers are likely, encountering the 'misty personage' of medieval romances and *The Waste Land*, to remember this fictional incarnation as a vigorous, 'spiky' personality and a trenchant talker. In the background are symbols – the ship, the voyage, the Roman Wall, the dance, the henge on Orkney and Arthur ('On this cruise we are in the midst of Arthur in more ways than one', says Professor Kopf, 30). There are degrees to which things can be known. The players understand the game of archetypes. Henchman is, poetically and psychologically, more enigmatic. Further back, in the recession of what can be known, are the great standing Stones of the Ring, against which Henchman is seen for the last time, 'built such a long time ago', symbolising mystery. The last sentence of the book recalls what Orkney was in the past and can still symbolise:

> On the far side of the waters, low rounded hills, soft and mysterious, concealed in luminous haze the frontiers of Thule: The edge of the known world; man's permitted limits; a green-barriered check-point, beyond which the fearful cataract of torrential seas cascaded down into Chaos.

These images reflect another aspect of Powell, the idea of mysterious and 'permitted' limits to the human world, with the implication of a design, requiring Henchman and Beals to meet on the *Alecto*, and implying something more than literary fun or a poetic personal – recognition rather than invention – in the archetype of Fisher King. If he can explore, in narrative and symbol, the edge of 'the known world' as Canon Fenneau understands the phrase, the novelist is himself a sort of mage. There is another edge of the known world: the human mind and personality. Powell would approve of the seventeenth-century concept of a magic realm within the mind matching the one beyond the reach of the senses. It is said of Louise Beals that she 'dwells' in 'an unmapped interior world of her own', its 'secret recesses' such that one cannot be sure about them (3). Personality is equally as mysterious as the mind. Mr Jack can be classified as a type of bore, in Theophrastian, classical terms which Powell accepts, but he is also a unique oddity, fascinating to the true student of mankind, as he is to Henchman. The description of him in the first two pages of Chapter 7 is an example of the comic art of explaining such oddity through writing, through the play of qualifications and admissions, constantly shifting as the narrator inspects the balance between Mr Jack's infinite seediness and his faint but relieving touches of humour and panache. Powell remains loyal to his principle that it is rampant, unredeemed will that damages people most. The wrecked figure of Mr Jack is more appealing than those of characters living on pure will, Lorna Tiptoft, Jilson, Lamont.

Notes

1. Volumes 1–9 first appeared as 'The Music of Time'.
2. See Douglas M. Davis, 'An Interview with Anthony Powell', *College English*, vol. 24 (April 1963) pp. 533–6; and *Faces in My Time* (Heinemann, 1980) pp. 134–7.
3. Michael Ratcliffe, 'Hearing Secret Harmonies', *The Times*, 6 September 1975, p. 6. See also, 'Anthony Powell: Some Questions Answered', a reply to a letter from Roland Mathias, *The Anglo-Welsh Review*, vol. 14 (1964) pp. 77–9, where Powell wrote: 'the novel is intended to be seen through the eyes of someone more or less like myself'.
4. *Infants of the Spring* (Heinemann, 1976) pp. 65, 67.
5. Ibid., p. 75.
6. Ibid., p. 83.
7. Ibid., p. 123.
8. Ibid., p. 152.
9. Ibid., p. 184.
10. *Messengers of Day* (Heinemann, 1978) p. 1.
11. Ibid., pp. 59–60.
12. Ibid., p. 21.
13. Ibid., p. 20.
14. *The Acceptance World*, Ch. 2 (Fontana edn, 1967) p. 38.
15. *Messengers of Day*, p. 18.
16. *Faces in My Time*, p. 66.
17. *Casanova's Chinese Restaurant*, Ch. 3 (Fontana edn, 1970) p. 165.
18. 'Proust as a Soldier', in *Marcel Proust 1871–1922: A Centenary Volume*, ed. Peter Quennell (Weidenfeld and Nicolson, 1971).
19. *The Strangers All Are Gone* (Heinemann, 1982) p. 186.
20. *Faces in My Time*, p. 103.
21. *Infants of the Spring*, p. 131.
22. *Messengers of Day*, p. 121.
23. Compare *At Lady Molly's*, Ch. 5 (Fontana edn, 1969) p. 211.
24. *Faces in My Time*, p. 88.
25. *The Strangers All Are Gone*, pp. 64–5.
26. *Faces in My Time*, p. 77.
27. *The Strangers All Are Gone*, pp. 28–33.
28. Ibid., p. 161.
29. Roy Fuller, 'Professors and Gods', *The Times Literary Supplement*, 9 March 1973, p. 274.

30. *The Strangers All Are Gone*, p. 159.
31. Ibid., p. 165.
32. *Hearing Secret Harmonies*, Ch. 4 (Fontana edn, 1977) p. 119.
33. *Casanova's Chinese Restaurant*, Ch. 1, p. 20.
34. *Faces in My Time*, p. 172.
35. *The Military Philosophers*, Ch. 4 (Fontana edn, 1971) pp. 189–90.
36. Ibid., p. 190.
37. See interview in *College English*, vol. 24, p. 534.
38. Powell's preface to *The Album of Anthony Powell's Dance to the Music of Time*, ed. Violet Powell (Thames and Hudson, 1987) p. 7.
39. *The Soldier's Art*, Ch. 1 (Fontana edn, 1968) p. 27.
40. *Messengers of Day*, p. 82.
41. The (anonymous) reviewer for *The Times Literary Supplement*, 17 September 1931, suggested that 'Palindrome' applies to the whole novel.
42. Powell's preface to *Handbook to Anthony Powell's Dance to the Music of Time*, ed. Hilary Spurling (Heinemann, 1977) p. vii.
43. *Spectator*, 24 January 1936, p. 144.
44. See interview with W. J. Weatherby, *The Twentieth Century*, July 1961, p. 51.
45. 'Marriage à la Mode – 1936', *Spectator*, 24 June 1960, p. 919.
46. 'The Bored Barbarians', *New Statesman*, 25 June 1960, pp. 947–8.
47. *Books Do Furnish a Room*, Ch. 4 (Fontana edn, 1972) p. 157. 'Personal myth' is one of the General's psychoanalytical terms: 'it is not what happens to people that is significant, but what they think happens to them'. Jenkins uses 'myth' in other senses.
48. *Casanova's Chinese Restaurant*, Ch. 1, p. 9; *At Lady Molly's*, Ch. 1 (first paragraph).
49. Powell says that he had in mind Hubert Duggan's resemblance to 'the central figure in crimson' when he wrote, in Ch. 1 of *A Question of Upbringing*, that Stringham resembled Alexander in Veronese's picture; he learned later that the National Gallery identifies this figure as Alexander's comrade Hephaistion: 'others disagree with this judgment, and I am with them, until convinced by overwhelming iconography' (*Infants of the Spring*, pp. 99–100).
50. Powell consulted the Welsh actor and dramatist Alun Owen, who found 'nothing inherently wrong' in the Welsh dialogue of *The Valley of Bones* and *The Soldier's Art*; above all, Owen said, the dialogue reproduced 'what the Narrator heard' (*Faces in My Time*, p. 101).
51. Rochester's 'Upon a Drinking Bowl' is a free version of the 18th Ode of Anacreon. English troops took part in the French capture of the Dutch fort of Maastricht in July 1673; a mock performance of the siege was staged at the English court a year later. Yarmouth Leaguer was a base camp for the campaign against Holland in 1673–4. The boys whose limbs are entwined are Cupid and Bacchus.
52. See the epigraph to *Afternoon Men* for Robert Burton's reference to the enchanted horn of Astolpho in Ariosto; this makes another link between the last volume of *Dance* and Powell's first novel.
53. *New Statesman*, 25 June 1960, pp. 947–8.

54. Interview with Alan Brownjohn, 'Profile 6', *The New Review*, vol. 1, no. 6 (September 1974) p. 25.
55. See the last page of *Faces in My Time*.
56. See interview with W. J. Weatherby, *The Twentieth Century*, July 1961, pp. 50–3.
57. Peter Conrad, *The Everyman History of English Literature* (J. M. Dent, 1985) pp. 691–3.
58. 'Degrees of Decay', *The Times Literary Supplement*, 22 June 1973, p. 709.
59. 'Afternoon World', review of *The Acceptance World*, *Spectator*, 13 May 1955.
60. *The Strangers All Are Gone*, p. 14.

Select Bibliography

The place of publication, unless stated, is London.

WORKS BY ANTHONY POWELL

(i) NOVELS

Afternoon Men (Duckworth, 1931; Heinemann, 1952; New York: Holt, 1932).

Venusberg (Duckworth, 1932; Harmondsworth: Penguin, 1961; New York: Periscope Holliday, 1952).

From a View to a Death (Duckworth, 1933; Heinemann, 1945; as *Mr Zouch: Superman: From a View to a Death*, New York: Vanguard Press, 1934).

Agents and Patients (Duckworth, 1936; Heinemann, 1955; Harmondsworth: Penguin, 1961; New York: Periscope Holliday, 1952).

What's Become of Waring (Cassell, 1939; Heinemann, 1953; Boston: Little Brown, 1963).

A Dance to the Music of Time

A Question of Upbringing (Heinemann, and New York: Scribner, 1951).

A Buyer's Market (Heinemann, 1952; New York: Scribner, 1953).

The Acceptance World (Heinemann, 1955; New York: Farrar Strauss, 1956).

At Lady Molly's (Heinemann, 1957; Boston: Little Brown, 1958).

Casanova's Chinese Restaurant (Heinemann, and Boston: Little Brown, 1960).

The Kindly Ones (Heinemann, and Boston: Little Brown, 1962).

The Valley of Bones (Heinemann, and Boston: Little Brown, 1964).

The Soldier's Art (Heinemann, and Boston: Little Brown, 1966).

The Military Philosophers (Heinemann, 1968; Boston: Little Brown, 1969).

Books Do Furnish a Room (Heinemann, and Boston: Little Brown, 1971).

Temporary Kings (Heinemann, and Boston: Little Brown, 1973).

Hearing Secret Harmonies (Heinemann, 1975; Boston: Little Brown, 1976).

All volumes of *A Dance to the Music of Time* are available in paperback in Fontana Books, and New York: Warner Books.

O, How the Wheel Becomes It! (Heinemann, 1983; Harmondsworth: Penguin, 1984; New York: Hold Rinehart, 1983).

The Fisher King (Heinemann, 1986; Sceptre Books, 1987; New York: Norton, 1986).

(ii) PLAYS

Two Plays: The Garden God, and The Rest I'll Whistle (Heinemann, 1971; Boston: Little Brown, 1972).

(iii) VERSE

Caledonia: A Fragment (privately printed [1934]; collected in *The New Oxford Book of Light Verse*, ed. Kingsley Amis, Oxford: Oxford University Press, 1978, pp. 245–9).

(iv) AUTOBIOGRAPHY

To Keep the Ball Rolling: The Memoirs of Anthony Powell (4 vols)

Infants of the Spring (Heinemann, and New York: Holt Rinehart, 1977).

Messengers of Day (Heinemann, and New York: Holt Rinehart, 1978).

Faces in My Time (Heinemann, 1980; New York: Holt Rinehart, 1981).

The Strangers All Are Gone (Heinemann, 1982; New York: Holt Rinehart, 1983).

To Keep the Ball Rolling: The Memoirs of Anthony Powell (abridged edition, Harmondsworth: Penguin, 1983; New York: Penguin, 1984).

(v) OTHER

John Aubrey and His Friends (Heinemann, and New York: Scribner, 1948; revised, Heinemann, and New York: Barnes and Noble, 1963).

Barnard Letters 1778–1824 (ed.) (Duckworth, 1928).

Novels of High Society from the Victorian Age (ed.) (Pilot Press, 1947).

Brief Lives and Other Selected Writings of John Aubrey (ed.) (Cresset Press, and New York: Scribner, 1949).

(vi) INTERVIEWS

Brownjohn, Alan, 'Anthony Powell, A Profile', *The New Review*, vol. 1 (September 1974) no. 6.

Davis, Douglas M., 'An Interview with Anthony Powell: Frome, England, June 1962', *College English*, vol. 24 (April 1963) pp. 533–6.

Shakespeare, Nicholas, *The Times*, 3 April 1986, p. 15.

Weatherby, W. J., 'Taken from Life', *The Twentieth Century*, vol. 170, no. 1010 (July 1961) pp. 50–3.

SECONDARY CRITICISM

(i) CRITICAL BOOKS

Bergonzi, Bernard, *Anthony Powell* (Harlow: Longman, 1962; revised 1971).

Bergonzi, Bernard, *The Situation of the Novel* (Macmillan, 1970; revised 1979).

Brennan, Neil, *Anthony Powell* (New York: Twayne, 1974).

McEwan, Neil, *The Survival of the Novel: British Fiction in the Later Twentieth Century* (Macmillan, and New York: Barnes and Noble, 1981).

Morris, Robert K., *The Novels of Anthony Powell* (Pittsburgh: University of Pittsburgh Press, 1968).

Russell, John, *Anthony Powell: A Quintet, Sextet and War* (Bloomington: Indiana University Press, 1970).

Tucker, James, *The Novels of Anthony Powell* (Macmillan, and New York: Columbia University Press, 1976).

(ii) CRITICAL ARTICLES

Bayley, John, 'A Family and its Fictions', *The Times Literary Supplement*, 12 September 1975, pp. 1011–13.

Brooke, Jocelyn, 'From Wauchop to Widmerpool', *London Magazine*, vol. 7 (1960) no. 9, pp. 60–4.

Hall, James, 'The Uses of Polite Surprise: Anthony Powell', *Essays in Criticism*, vol. 12 (April 1962) pp. 167–83.

Karl, Frederick, 'Sisyphus Descending: Mythical Patterns in the Novels of Anthony Powell', *Mosaic* (Winnipeg), vol. 4 (1971) no. 3.

Larkin, Philip, 'Mr Powell's Mural', *New Statesman*, 19 February 1971, pp. 243–4.

McCall, Raymond G., 'Anthony Powell's Gallery', *College English*, vol. 27 (December 1965) pp. 227–35.

Mizener, Arthur, 'A Dance to the Music of Time: the Novels of Anthony Powell', *Kenyon Review*, vol. 22 (1960) pp. 79–92.

Wall, Stephen, 'Aspects of the Novel, 1930–1960', in Bernard Bergonzi (ed.), *History of Literature in the English Language*, vol. vii: *The Twentieth Century* (Barrie and Jenkins, 1970) pp. 237–41.

(iii) HANDBOOK

Spurling, Hilary, *Handbook to Anthony Powell's Dance to the Music of Time* (Heinemann, 1977; as *Invitation to the Dance: A Guide to Anthony Powell's Dance to the Music of Time*, Boston: Little Brown, 1978).

(iv) ALBUM

The Album of Anthony Powell's Dance to the Music of Time, ed. Violet Powell, preface by Anthony Powell, introduction by John Bayley (Thames and Hudson, 1987).

Index